T0319081

ON THE PRINCIPLES AND PRACTICE OF CONDUCTING

MARKAND THAKAR

ON THE PRINCIPLES AND PRACTICE OF CONDUCTING

UNIVERSITY OF ROCHESTER PRESS

First published 2016
Reprinted in paperback 2024

University of Rochester Press
668 Mt. Hope Avenue, Rochester, NY 14620, USA
www.urpress.com
and Boydell & Brewer Limited
PO Box 9, Woodbridge, Suffolk IP12 3DF, UK
www.boydellandbrewer.com

ISBN-13: 978-1-58046-540-3 (hardcover)
ISBN-13: 978-1-64825-096-5 (paperback)

Library of Congress Cataloging-in-Publication Data

Names: Thakar, Markand, 1955– author.
Title: On the principles and practice of conducting / Markand Thakar.
Description: Rochester, NY : University of Rochester Press, 2016. | 2016 |
Includes bibliographical references and index.
Identifiers: LCCN 2016003684 | ISBN 9781580465403 (hardcover : alkaline
    paper)
Subjects: LCSH: Conducting—Instruction and study.
Classification: LCC MT85 .T43 2016 | DDC 781.45—dc23 LC record available at
    http://lccn.loc.gov/2016003684

A catalogue record for this title is available from the British Library.

dedicated with love to Oliver, who inspires me daily

He felt that the spirit of beauty had folded him round like a mantle and that in reverie at least he had been acquainted with nobility.

—James Joyce, *A Portrait of the Artist as a Young Man*

CONTENTS

PREFACE

Music can be beautiful. It can move us, it can exalt us, it can make us better. It offers a transcendent experience of the essence of our selves, one that affirms and strengthens us in our everyday lives. Such an experience is literally transcendent: in our consciousness of the sounds we become the sounds; we transcend the duality that exists between us and them. Beauty—which can occur at different levels of the consciousness and to different degrees—exists to the extent that we experience this transcendence.

In my previous book, *Looking for the "Harp" Quartet: An Investigation into Musical Beauty* (Rochester, NY: University of Rochester Press, 2011), I explored the contributions to that experience by the listener, who absorbs sounds; the composer, who suggests them; and the performer, who brings them to life. The conductor guides an ensemble of performers in that undertaking. But how?

In one common understanding, the composition is a script inviting diverse realizations by creative interpreters, the ensemble is a collection of individuals with divergent musical sensibilities and instincts, and the job of the conductor is to visit a unifying interpretation on the group. In another, the composition is a definitive text, the ensemble is a collection of willing but imperfect souls, and the conductor's job is to honor the composer by ensuring the requisite reading. Both understandings require a controlling figure, called a "director," "chief," and even "military commander" in Latin, Germanic, Slavic, and Asian languages. Both assume the musicians' responsibility is to respond to the demands of that controlling figure.

On the Principles and Practice of Conducting is grounded in a different understanding of the process and thus of the function of the conductor. In actuality, an ensemble is a collection of essentially like-minded beings with an inherent inclination to come together and a proclivity to respond to the demands of the sounds in the same or similar ways. In fact, the most beautiful, most moving experience requires a limited range of conditions in sound: a limited range of the temporal placement of tones that we perceive or can perceive as simultaneous; a limited range of pitch that we all perceive or can perceive as in tune, similarly a limited range of tempo, a limited range of phrasing inflections, and a limited range of global tempo direction (pacing) that we all perceive or can perceive.

Conducting a body of sentient musicians, we are not—as the driver of a car—in complete control of speed and direction; rather, we are like the equestrian: with shared sensibilities we guide and influence, by conforming the rhythms of our physical motions to those of the living, breathing organism. At best the conductor can join with the musicians in responding to the demands of the sounds, confirming and synchronizing and guiding them to a shared purpose. A musician responding to the demands of the sounds rather than to the demands of the stick is much the better one, and so the English *conductor*—a transmitter of energy—is much the better term.[1]

On Conducting attempts to answer the question "But how?" Chapter 1 concerns the responsibility of the conductor for understanding the conditions in sound necessary for the most beautiful, most moving, most transcendent experiences. It addresses dynamic structure and balance, two of the performer's responsibilities treated in far greater detail in *Looking for the "Harp" Quartet*. In fact, *On Conducting* is a kind of sequel for conductors to that earlier book; a concentrated working-through of *"Harp" Quartet* would be a helpful prelude to undertaking this one. Making beautiful music is overwhelmingly the conductor's most important responsibility; a conductor who comes to the podium without an understanding of how the tones can come to life to allow the most moving experience is sorely deficient.

Chapter 2 discusses the necessity of focusing the consciousness on all the sounds and only the sounds, as well as the critical issue of trust. Hearing everything has a particular bearing on finding a tempo and on rehearsing. Chapter 3 discusses the function of the conductor, the value of physical alignment and balance, and the importance of using only the muscles necessary. The chapter also presents the three fundamental conducting

---

[1]   We absorb and collect and contribute and transmit energy throughout the entire body of musicians. To be sure, as the most influential musician onstage, the conductor's contribution is determinative within the range of conditions that allow a sublime performance; and different sublime performances within that range will necessarily be unique.

patterns, and it identifies the particular muscles that generate the motions of arms and hands through each of those patterns.

Finally, chapter 4 describes in detail how the conductor can join the freed mind and freed body to the sounds, ultimately our highest, most effective, most rewarding modus operandi. It discusses conforming the beat gesture to the character of the musical beat, to the shape of the phrase, to the overall volume, and to the quality of sound.

Addendum A addresses the technical challenges of starting works or movements, of ending them, and of conducting fermatas. Addendum B deals with assorted issues large and small that arise in the curious process of using physical gestures to aid the making of music by an ensemble.

On Conducting is at essence a practical manual for building musical understanding and physical skills, intended for anyone who picks up a baton or stands on a podium with the intention of helping an ensemble make music: a great symphony orchestra or a church choir or a middle-school wind ensemble. It is offered to serve a classroom of beginners or to provide a path to growth for an advanced student or even an experienced professional.

Each chapter begins with underlying principles; most include PRACTICAL MATTERS,[2] discussions of real-life applications, and EXERCISES for developing skills. Occasionally, ESSENTIAL PRINCIPLES are highlighted. A website, www.markandthakar.com/OnConducting, offers links to video demonstrations of the exercises in chapter 3 and chapter 4, as noted in the text. It also offers downloadable scores and parts, available for a mélange of transposing and non-transposing instruments, which allows for hands-on experience conducting a group of friends or the often motley group of instrumentalists found in conducting classes.

The material of *On Conducting* is interrelated: a thorough grasp of any chapter will be informed and enhanced by a thorough grasp of the others (which has made organizing it into sequential book form challenging). I have long considered shampoo bottle instructions to use, rinse, and repeat the sign of a defective product. Nonetheless, I find myself suggesting something similar: work through the book, live it, and work through it again. May you prevail over its defects, may you venture forth cleansed of any occluded consciousness and scrubbed of any unnecessary tension, and with a free mind and a free body may you empower the musicians in your care to their most magical, most beautiful efforts.

---

2   Practical matters in two senses, as practical applications most certainly matter.

ACKNOWLEDGMENTS

This effort owes considerably to the contributions of a substantial number of friends, colleagues, and students. For providing me with an education in anatomy, I wish to thank two medical professionals—Drs. Stacey H. Berner, MD, and Stephen Bender, DC—as well as Peter Jacobson, a fine conductor who is also a certified Alexander Technique teacher, and Janette LaBarre, also a fine conductor who is a licensed massage therapist.

I wish to thank the esteemed Sydney Meshkov for his assistance with matters of physics. I am grateful to Oliver I. Thakar for producing the beat diagrams that appear in chapter 4, and I am especially appreciative of Philip R. Emory, who worked long and hard creating the pattern diagrams that appear in chapters 3 and 4.

The associated video demonstrations available at www.markandthakar .com/OnConducting were produced by Dennis Drenner, with much-appreciated financial assistance from the Peabody Conservatory.

I most gratefully acknowledge Ralph Locke for his belief in the project and helpful prodding; Julia Cook for her helpful oversight; Cheryl Carnahan for her "un-comma-promising" commitment; Susan Baron for her tireless editing; and, for their invaluable and sundry wisdom, advice, and assistance, Dennis Báthory-Kitsz, James Chang, Matthew Faerber, Piotr Gajewski, Grant Gilman, Tomasz Golka, Joshua Hong, Alexander Kahn, Dario Macellari, Timothy McDonnell, Stephanie McGurren, Andrew Monticello, John Moran, Dominique Røyem, Hannah Schendel, Mark Shapiro, Paul H. Smith, Rebecca Smithorn, Brian Stone, James Stopher, Duain Wolfe, and Jenny Ching Yee Wong.

Finally, I ask forgiveness from all those students—too numerous to name—to whom I have delivered misinformation over the years with the absolute self-assuredness of a conductor, and from the musicians whom I have led astray too often to count.

CHAPTER ONE

MAKE BEAUTIFUL MUSIC

Involving Singularity of Tones in Succession and of Tones Sounding Simultaneously

A space alien comes to town.

"Gee, Earth," the alien says, "nice place you got here. What do you do for fun?"

"Well, um, we go to concerts," you say.

The alien asks "What's a concert?"

"Well," you say, "there's a big room, and a bunch of people go in and sit down. The lights go out, and in a corner of the room some people make noises."

"How strange! Gosh, how long do you have to do that?" asks the alien.

"Oh, we do it for about two hours," you answer.

"My goodness," says the alien. "So they must pay you?"

"Oh no, we pay a handsome sum."

"OK then, I have just one question . . ." the alien pauses, "Why?"

Why indeed!

Experience of Beauty

The experience of beauty is an act of the consciousness. Ordinary acts of human consciousness are characterized by an inherent dichotomy between the "me" and the "not me." There's a table there, and I'm not the table. There's a computer there, and I'm not the computer. I'm not the couch, the lamp, or the rug. I'm not the window, the shade, the light, or the heat. I'm not the revolving door, the Industrial Revolution, the Revolutionary War. I'm not détente, entente, Immanuel Kant, or Garamond font. I am not the innumerable phenomena—things and concepts—external to me.

Aesthetic experience—the experience of beauty—is different. I see a painting. I absorb the images. I take them in. I lose myself in the images. It is a magical, transcendent experience, one in which I transcend that duality between me and the images. Or I go to a concert. The sounds wash over me. I absorb the sounds. I take them in. I lose myself in the sounds. I become the sounds. In this literally transcendent experience, I transcend the duality that exists between me and the sounds. I have become the sounds, not in physical reality of course, but in this act of my consciousness there is no subject and no object.

So why do we go to concerts? Because under certain circumstances we can have a transcendent, life-affirming experience: just by absorbing sound we can transcend the duality that exists between the self and the external world. We can be in touch with the very essence of ourselves, we can be affirmed, we can be moved, we can be exalted. We can be better.

Any musical experience has two components: the subject—the listener—and the object—the sounds. To transcend the self/external world duality, the listener must be fully open to the sounds . . . to all the sounds and only the sounds. To only the sounds, because a consciousness of the sounds *and* something else brings with it the duality between self and external world. If, for example, my consciousness is taken up with the cellist's dress or with a thought of the last time I heard the work or with how this performance compares to the Toscanini recording, I am different from that dress, which is external to me; I am different from that Toscanini recording, which is external to me; and I am different from that previous performance experience.

And the listener must be open to all the sounds. If my consciousness is focused on less than the totality of the sounds—for example, on the clarinet melody only or on the brass section only—the self is necessarily a component of that conscious act. I choose to limit the object on which I focus, and I choose the specific nature of that limitation. It results in the same self/external object duality: I, here, am limiting the object of my attention to the clarinet or to the brass section, out there.

Tones in Succession

For the listener to absorb a succession of sounds in a singular act of consciousness, those sounds must allow it; the succession must be perceivable as singular. Achieving singularity is a commonly understood goal for performers, for example, singularity of pitch and ensemble: we play in tune to experience the magical sound of multiple tones participating in one pure sonority; we play with good ensemble to be captivated by multiple tones participating in a single metric system. That said, the overarching element that ties together a succession of tones into a singular object is the structure of energy.[1]

As an example of how energy functions in the physical world, consider the motion of a simple pendulum, such as a child's swing. I give the child a single push. She swings back and forth, lower and lower each time, until she comes to rest. To keep her swinging at the same height, I give her a small push each time she returns to me. I get her swinging higher and higher by giving increasingly harder pushes. As soon as I stop pushing, though, the height decreases with each swing until the child comes to rest at the lowest point.

In terms of physics, the simple pendulum is in a state of equilibrium. By giving a push I apply a force, which injects energy into the swing. It oscillates. With each oscillation the amplitude decreases, as the energy is converted to heat by friction with the swing mechanism and the air. Eventually all the energy is dissipated, and the swing returns to equilibrium. To keep it oscillating at the same amplitude I must apply a new force with each oscillation, injecting energy: exactly as much energy as had been dissipated. To increase the amplitude, I must apply more force with each oscillation, injecting more energy than had been dissipated. When I stop injecting energy, the amplitude decreases as energy is dissipated with each oscillation. When all the energy is dissipated, the swing returns to equilibrium.

Sound in a musical context works in a similar way. The equilibrium of sound is silence: a sound exists only to the extent that it successfully resists

---

[1] The discussion of energy in music in the subsequent paragraphs is largely synopsized from the extensive exploration in Thakar, *"Harp" Quartet*, which occurs particularly in four chapters: the dialogue and article on the composer's contribution (chapters 3 and 7) and the dialogue and article on the performer's contribution (chapters 4 and 8).

the inevitable return to silence. Imagine a pizzicato violin tone (example 1.1). The plucking injects energy into the string, which vibrates, creating a sound. As the energy in the string converts to heat, the sound dissipates with the decreasing amplitude of the vibrations, returning to silence. We can prevent the sound from subsiding by continuing to apply force, for example, by bowing the string (example 1.2), which maintains the vibrations at the same amplitude. We can also increase the force by increasing the volume with added pressure and speed of the bow (example 1.3), thus increasing the amplitude of the vibrations. As soon as we stop applying force, the amplitude of vibrations begins to decrease, and the sound dissipates until it returns to silence.

Example 1.1.   Example 1.2.   Example 1.3.

In considering how sound acts on us, it is critical to note that sound does not exist in physical reality. In physical reality a force (a vibrating object) injects energy into the air, creating waves (compressions and rarefactions of air molecules) that get translated into sound in the brain. Sound exists only in our consciousness of it. Just as a push is a force injecting energy into the swing, a sound in a musical context is a force injecting energy into the consciousness.

Consider that pizzicato tone: it is a force against silence. As we experience it, it injects a degree of energy into our consciousness. To increase that energy in our consciousness we can increase the volume: a louder tone is a stronger force that conflicts with silence to a greater degree and thus injects more energy (example 1.3). We can also increase the energy in our consciousness with rhythmic density: increasing the speed—and thus the rhythmic density of the tones—builds energy (example 1.4).

Example 1.4.

We can also increase the energy with pitch (example 1.5).

Example 1.5.

And we can increase the energy with harmony (example 1.6).

Example 1.6.

Each vibration of the string is a force that moves air molecules, resulting in a sound. As the string continues to vibrate at successively smaller amplitudes, each smaller vibration is a force that results in a successively softer sound, until there is no more force and the sound is fully dissipated. In a musical context, energy in the consciousness works in a similar way: the energy is released over time—often by decreasing injections of force—until it is fully dissipated or resolved. A musical object comes to us as singular if the energy it creates is resolved *consequently*: in other words, if no music is left after the energy has been depleted and—to the extent possible—no energy is left at the end of the music. A resolution that releases all the energy created within a grouping (to the extent possible) is consequent; it is a consequence of the impulse that precedes it.

EXERCISES: Consequent Resolutions

1. Perform example 1.7, taking note of both the energy created by the initial ascending fourth and the consequent resolution of that energy offered by the final five tones.

    Example 1.7.

    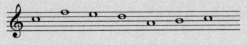

2. Perform example 1.8, taking note of both the additional energy created by the initial ascending sixth (as compared to the ascending fourth of example 1.7) and the longer consequent resolution of the final nine tones.

Example 1.8.

3. Example 1.9 illustrates a line in which the energy ends well before the music. Perform the example, taking note of the energy created by the initial ascending sixth and noting when that energy is fully released.

Example 1.9.

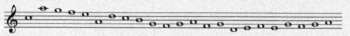

4. Example 1.10 illustrates energy incompletely resolved. Perform the example, taking note of the energy created by the initial ascending sixth and then of the energy that continues unresolved after the final tone.

Example 1.10.

5. The progression of four-part chords in example 1.11 illustrates the creation of energy from harmonic tension. Perform the example, taking note of the energy that grows through the fourth harmony.

Example 1.11.

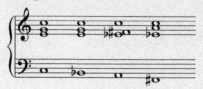

6. Add chords to the succession of four-part chords in example 1.11, such that the energy can be resolved consequently. Perform it, creating energy and resolving it consequently. Then repeat the exercise with too great a resolution—that is, with too many additional chords—so the energy dies before the end of the progression. Finally, repeat the exercise with too few additional chords to resolve the energy consequently.
7. Example 1.12 illustrates how energy is created by increasing rhythmic density (as example 1.4 above), as well as how that energy is resolved by decreasing rhythmic density. Clap the top line of 1.12 at a steady volume, taking note of the energy growing as a result of the increased rhythmic density. Now perform the complete example, gradually increasing and then decreasing the rhythmic density, such that the energy created is resolved consequently.

Example 1.12.

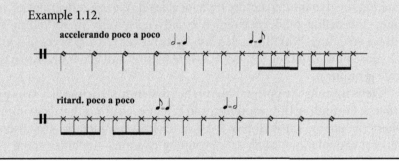

Inflections of Volume and Tempo (the Performer's Contribution)

The sounds result from contributions by the composer and the performer, and each has a role in creating the dynamic structure (the structure of energy).[2] The composer has four principal tools to create and resolve energy: volume, melodic line (pitch), harmony, and rhythmic density. Increasing the

---

[2] In the term *dynamic structure*, the word *dynamic* refers to energy and not to inflections of volume—i.e., dynamics. The dynamic structure of a grouping of tones is the creation and release of energy in our experience of that grouping.

volume, the height of the line, the harmonic tension, or the rhythmic density tends to build energy; decreasing them over time tends to resolve it.[3] The composition presents the performer with a skeletal framework for a hierarchical dynamic structure: motives, within phrases, within periods, within sections, and so on. *The performer creates the dynamic structure, which results from the experience of sounds.* The most beautiful performance requires a singular dynamic structure at all levels of the hierarchy. A phrase—itself a musical object—comes to us as singular if the energy created within it is resolved consequently. The same is true of the next level of the hierarchy, perhaps a grouping of two or three phrases: that grouping will come to us as singular if the energy created within it is played out to the extent possible. In continuation, this is the case for every level of the hierarchy, up to and including the entire movement.[4]

While composers have four principal tools to contribute to the creation of the dynamic structure, performers have only two: volume and rhythmic density. Increasing either tends to build energy; decreasing them over time tends to release it. Volume is our predominant tool in creating the dynamic structure on a local level. We use inflections of volume—increasing or decreasing—virtually constantly in unfolding the phrase structure. Rhythmic density—getting faster or slower—is by far the more powerful tool; we use it less frequently and generally for larger-scale groupings.

Determining the optimal hierarchic dynamic structure is a two-part process: (1) finding the groupings, and (2) for each grouping, determining where the energy must climax to be resolved consequently. Any discrete musical articulation—such as a grouping of tones—includes some creation of energy and some resolution of that energy. The grouping begins where the energy begins to increase, and after some degree of resolution it ends with the *next* increase of energy. Finding the grouping structure of a succession of tones is a trial-and-error process that involves gauging inherent tendencies of the tones. And it may be a reciprocal process, in

---

[3]   Other tools of the composer, such as timbre or articulations, have a minimal effect on the dynamic structure.

[4]   This is "to the extent possible" because in fact almost no grouping on any level of the hierarchy of a masterwork allows for the complete release of the energy. If 100 percent of the energy were released, there would be no connection of that grouping to the larger whole. Perhaps surprisingly, this is true even at the end of a movement, where energy carries over minimally past the sounding of the final tone. In recognition of this minimal carryover of energy at the end of movements, composers—for example, Mozart, Beethoven, and Mendelssohn—added extra bars of rest or added fermatas over the final double bars or final rests. Exceptions—works in which the energy ends completely with the final sound—are those that release the final sound ever so gradually, such as Barber's *Adagio for Strings* or the final movement of Dvořák's Symphony no. 9 ("From the New World").

that the boundaries of the groupings are often dependent on how the energy can be created and resolved. In other words, step 1 is determining the grouping structure. Step 2 is finding the climax of each grouping, but in the process it may be necessary to return to step 1 to reconfigure the grouping structure.

Example 1.13a.

Example 1.13a represents the opening eight bars of the Trio from Mozart's *Eine kleine Nachtmusik*, movement 3, "Menuetto." Elements that tend to build energy are the soprano ascent to the high D and the increased rhythmic density of bass motion in bars 5–8; elements that tend to resolve it are the soprano descent from the high D to the final D of bar 8 and the contracting distance between bass and soprano.

In finding the grouping structure, we are likely to begin by assuming the ascent to the high D has some kind of climactic function. However, if we use volume to climax the energy with the downbeat of bar 2 and listen carefully to the resultant structure of energy, we find it insufficient to carry through the entire eight bars. One solution might be to move the climax later, perhaps to the downbeat of bar 3, by increasing the volume to that point. With the climax at the downbeat of bar 3, we could decrease the volume to the end of bar 8, but the resultant energy is still insufficient to carry to the end of the passage. Or we could decrease the volume for a bar or two and then increase the volume in line with the inherent tendency to increase energy in the final four bars, in which case we find that too much energy remains at the end of bar 8. Ultimately—perhaps after much trial and error—we come to understand that to be heard as singular (such that to the extent possible the energy and the music end at the same time), the eight bars must be unfolded in two four-bar groupings. In the first, the energy must climax with the downbeat of bar 2 and be resolved through the end of bar 4; in the second, the energy must climax with the soprano E of bar 7 and be resolved through the end of bar 8. The black triangles of example 1.13b illustrate level *a* of the hierarchy of dynamic structure: the two four-bar groupings, as well as the dynamic structure required for each to be heard as singular.

Example 1.13b.

Groupings are hierarchic. Finding the next level of the hierarchy involves the same two-step process: determining the grouping structure, then determining the structure of energy such that the energy created can be resolved. In this case step 1 is clear: the two four-bar groupings join into a single eight-bar phrase. Performing this larger eight-bar grouping using volume to create the dynamic structure, we find that to make one singular unit, the energy must climax with the bar 2 downbeat. The climax at bar 7 is secondary and sustains the energy through the now six-bar resolution. This is illustrated by the level-b black triangles in example 1.13c.

Example 1.13c.

The overall volume of the passage is soft; the increase in volume to bar 2 is subtle, and the increase to bar 7 is minimal. Nonetheless, only within this hierarchic structure of energy—created by the performer's use of volume inflections—can these eight bars be absorbed as singular and thus within a single act of consciousness.

Example 1.14 presents a dynamic analysis of the German folksong "Hänschen Klein." Although it is a simple single-line tune, it is more complicated than the Mozart phrase above. Creating the dynamic structure necessary for a singular consciousness of all eight bars entails an additional level of hierarchy and requires the tool of rhythmic density in addition to volume.

Example 1.14.

Level *a* represents the dynamic structure necessary for groupings to be resolved consequently on a local level, with the addition of the sub-impulses in bars 1, 3, and 7. Level *b* represents the next level of the hierarchy, the two four-bar phrases in which the height of the energy must come with the third-bar downbeat to be resolved consequently. And level *c* represents the overall dynamic structure of the entire tune, which climaxes with the second of the two level-*b* climaxes, at bar 7.

However, it would be impossible to perform the final four-bar grouping in tempo without excess energy remaining. So, ending the music and the energy at the same time requires the other tool of rhythmic density: the speed must be decreased subtly in the final bar to allow time for the energy to play out fully.[5]

---

[5] A more comprehensive discussion of the process of this dynamic analysis follows: level a of black triangles illustrates the dynamic structure that enables the first-level groupings to be heard as singular. Bar 1 encompasses two mini-groupings of three notes; in each the energy must climax with the first note, and the entire one-bar grouping climaxes with the downbeat G. A second grouping encompasses bars 2 and 3; the climax of this two-bar grouping comes with the downbeat G of bar 3. Bar 4 consists of its own grouping; to be heard as singular the climax must come with the downbeat C. Bar 5 consists of a single grouping that ends with the beginning of bar 6; bars 6 and 7 combine into a grouping that climaxes with the downbeat G of bar 7, and bar 8 is a repetition of the bar-4 grouping. We make this dynamic structure with inflections of volume. Level b illustrates the next-level dynamic structure, which we again make primarily with volume. The first four bars join into a single grouping in which the climax must come with the downbeat of bar 3; this climactic bar 3 is louder than the climax of bar 1. Bars 3 and 4 combine to resolve this climax, with each of the three component groupings beginning successively softer. Similarly, bars 5–8 join into a single four-bar grouping, in which the climax comes with the downbeat of bar 7. Level c illustrates the dynamic structure necessary for the entire eight bars to be heard as singular. We might have considered making the bar-3 climax stronger than the bar-7 climax. In that case the remaining bars would have to be a large-scale resolution, but there is not enough energy to carry through these final six bars. Thus the second climax at bar 7 must be the climax of the entire folksong, stronger than the climax at bar 3. The final two bars, which resolve the energy gathered over the first six bars, require a subtle ritardando or decreasing of the rhythmic density to allow the energy to end with the music.

The performer is responsible for the dynamic structure even when the composer specifies a dynamic or tempo inflection. Instead of determining *where* the height of the volume is or *whether* a ritard is necessary, our responsibility becomes the degree of inflection: how loud a sforzando or how great a ritard. The process, though, is the same.

Consider example 1.15, a dynamic analysis of the opening eight bars of Beethoven's Symphony no. 3 ("Eroica"), movement 2, in which the composer indicates a sforzando on the downbeat of bar 6. As illustrated in level *a*, the passage consists of three groupings: one encompassing the first two bars, climaxing with the soprano E♭ in bar 2; a second grouping encompassing bars 3 and 4, climaxing with the middle-voice F♯ that reaches up over the soprano line; and a third grouping encompassing the final four bars, climaxing with the soprano A♭ of bar 6. As illustrated in level *b*, the three groups are successively stronger; the climactic bar 6 serves as the climax of the entire eight-bar phrase. Beethoven indicates the climax with the sforzando on the bar-6 downbeat and the subsequent diminuendo. While the location of the climax is given, the performers have responsibility for how much climax—in other words, just how loud that sforzando must be.

Example 1.15.

EXERCISES: How Much Volume Inflection

1. Perform example 1.15 with a minimal sforzando, such that the energy dies before the end of the phrase.
2. Now perform the example with an extremely loud sforzando, such that the energy continues after the end of the phrase.
3. Now find the volume of sforzando that allows the energy and the music to end at the same time.

Example 1.16 presents a dynamic analysis of the first sixteen bars of the recapitulation of Beethoven's Symphony no. 5, movement 1, culminating with the out-of-tempo mini-cadenza in the oboe. As illustrated in level *a*, the passage consists of five groupings. One encompasses the first five bars, climaxing with the soprano C downbeat of bar 4; the C–E♭–C quarter notes of bars 4–5 form a sub-grouping. The second extends from the downbeat of bar 6 to the downbeat of bar 9, climaxing with the soprano D on the downbeat of bar 8; the G–B–G of bars 8–9 form another sub-grouping. Two 2-bar groupings follow, each climaxing on the soprano E♭. The final grouping encompasses bar 13 through the oboe solo; it climaxes with the *forte* G-major harmony.

Example 1.16.

As illustrated in level *b*, the climaxes of the five groups carry successively more energy, resulting from the rising pitch from grouping 1 through grouping 3, the contraction from four bars to the two bars of groupings 3 and 4, and finally the rising pitch and increasing volume of grouping 5. The *forte* G-major harmony climaxes the energy within the sixteen-bar phrase; the function of the oboe solo is to resolve the energy created in the previous fifteen bars. With the Adagio notation and the two fermatas, Beethoven specifies that this oboe line is to be out of tempo. While we know there must be extra time, how much extra time—in other words, how slow this Adagio must be—is the responsibility of the performers.[6]

EXERCISES: How Much Tempo Inflection

1. Perform example 1.16, stopping on the first fermata (omitting the oboe solo). Pay attention to the energy created, and take note of the point at which it dissipates.

---

[6] It is not uncommon for oboists to take too much time here, dissipating all the energy created well before the end of the passage.

2. Next, perform the full example. Play the oboe solo too slowly, so that all the energy is completely dissipated before the final fermata.
3. Now perform the full example, taking the oboe solo too fast to play out all the energy.
4. Finally, perform the full example, allowing the oboe solo to release all the accumulated energy, but not more.

EXERCISES: Finding the Optimal Dynamic Structure

1. Example 1.13c presents a dynamic analysis of the first eight bars of the Trio of Mozart's *Eine kleine Nachtmusik*, movement 3 "Menuetto." Complete a dynamic analysis of the entire twenty-bar Trio.
2. With a familiar tune (for example, a folksong or a Christmas carol), determine the hierarchical grouping structure: what are the groupings of the tones, what are the groupings of those groupings, and so on. Using volume and, if necessary, rhythmic density, try to perform the song such that each grouping within the hierarchy—up to and including that of the entire tune—creates energy and releases it to the extent possible.
3. Compose a melody and listen to how you must structure the energy using inflections of volume so the music and the energy end at the same time. If you find this impossible, amend your melody.
4. Harmonize the melody so it can be performed as a single overall grouping, with the energy and the music ending at the same time.

Simultaneous Tones

In addition to using volume to structure the energy in order to perceive sounds in succession as a singularity, we also use volume to structure the balance in order to perceive simultaneous sounds as a singularity. In balancing simultaneously sounding tones, the goal is a singular sound in which all the simultaneously sounding instruments participate distinctly (with primary melodic material having priority). Lack of a sublimely structured balance is as limiting to the possibility of transcending the multiplicity of sounds as is poor intonation or poor ensemble.

We structure simultaneous sounds to achieve a new, compound sound on the bases of register, of the inherent volume of the instrument, and of timbre. In blending paint to achieve a new color, we add the darker, more powerful color into the lighter one; similarly, in blending sounds, we blend the more powerful into the less powerful. More intense timbre is more powerful than less intense, louder is more powerful than softer, and lower register is more powerful than higher. Thus to achieve a new, compound sound in which multiple tones participate discretely, we blend the more intense timbre into the less intense, the louder-sounding instrument into the softer one, and the lower tone into the higher one.

Register is a critical consideration because of the acoustic phenomenon by which the ear assigns greater prominence to lower pitches. If two different pitches are produced at the same decibel level, the lower dominates the upper. Only if the lower pitch is physically softer than the upper can two discrete pitches join into a single new sound resulting from the equal participation of both.[7]

To create a singular object of multiple pitches, the tones must be prioritized from top to bottom: highest pitches loudest to lowest pitches softest. Consider a string section with the most common distribution: melodic priority in the first violins and successively lower pitches in the second violin, viola, cello, and bass sections. To produce a singular event out of the many sounding pitches, the second violins support the first violins at a slightly softer volume, loud enough to join but not loud enough to dominate; the violas support the second violins at a slightly softer volume, loud enough to join but not loud enough to dominate; the cellos support the violas; the basses support the cellos.

---

[7] How can a higher pitch carry more energy but sound softer than a simultaneous lower pitch? This seeming conflict results from the fundamental difference between the physical fact of frequency and the psychoacoustic phenomenon of masking. There is more inherent potential energy in the experience of a higher-pitched tone with its greater frequency than in that of a lower tone. And—as illustrated by equal loudness contours such as the Fletcher-Munson curve—the higher the pitch, the louder we experience a tone (up to about 4,000 Hz, or roughly three octaves above middle C). Nonetheless, when we experience multiple pitches sounding simultaneously, a lower tone masks a higher one; a higher tone does not mask a lower one. There is no conflict in the consequences for performing, however, as for both successions and simultaneities to be experienced as whole, upper tones must come to us as louder (absent other conflicting considerations).

A similar structure of volume would obtain in any ensemble of like instruments, such as a string trio, a quartet of recorders, or a chorus of voices. If the principal melodic material sounds in a voice other than the highest, the priority of volume remains loudest to softest as follows: principal melodic material, then the top voice of the accompaniment, then the next-highest pitch, and so on down to the lowest pitch.

Inherent volume of instruments is a key consideration in blending different sections of an ensemble. Consider a passage for an orchestra in which simultaneously sounding woodwinds, strings, brass, and percussion all have a dynamic marking of *forte*. If each instrument plays its own *forte*, the loudest instruments, the brass and percussion, will dominate and cover the softer strings, which will likely dominate and cover the softer woodwinds. All the tones can participate discretely only when strings play softly enough to join and support woodwinds, brasses play softly enough to join and support strings, and percussion instruments join and support brass.[8]

Timbre is another key consideration, especially in blending multiple instruments at the same pitch. Again, to create a new, compound timbre, we blend the more intense timbre into the less intense one. To blend a unison flute and oboe into a new, singular sound, the oboe plays softly enough to meld its sound into that of the flute. To create a new singular sound from a unison clarinet and bassoon, the bassoon plays softly enough to blend into the clarinet.

In blending tones with conflicting considerations, register is always the priority. For example, consider the English horn and muted trumpet in octaves in the first movement of Claude Debussy's *La Mer* at bar 9. To create a new, compound timbre out of the two, we blend the lower, more intense English horn into the higher, less intense trumpet. In this and in all situations in which multiple tones blend into a new sound, the softer tone is just minimally softer; it fits snugly right up inside the higher-priority tone.

---

[8]   This is assuming a common arrangement in which the principal melodic material sounds in the first violins and upper woodwinds and the remainder of the instruments have an accompanying or secondary function.

PRACTICAL MATTER: Play the Entire Ensemble

An ensemble necessarily lacks cohesiveness or singularity when the individual members do not incorporate all the sounds of the ensemble in their consciousnesses. Rather than instruct individual musicians—"you louder, you softer, etc."—consider asking all the musicians to feel as if they are creating the entire collective sound; in other words, playing the whole orchestra and not just their own parts. The results in cohesiveness can be remarkable.

EXERCISE: Power of Lower Tones

Have two instruments play tones an octave apart at a moderate volume. Have the lower tone increase in volume, and ask listeners to indicate when they no longer hear the upper one. Now start again with the two tones an octave apart. This time have the upper tone increase in volume, and ask listeners to indicate when they no longer hear the lower tone. (Hint: they will *never* not hear the lower tone!)

EXERCISES: Balance

1. With a piano (or other variable-volume instrument), play each of the dyads of example 1.17, and experiment with different structures of volume until the two join into one. Take note of the relative volume of the individual tones.

   Example 1.17.

2. Repeat the exercise, singing one of the tones and playing the other.
3. Example 1.18 presents three-voice chords resulting from adding a tone to the dyads above. Perform the same exercises as above, playing the chord with different structures of volume until the three join into one. Take note of the relative volume of the three individual tones.

Example 1.18.

4. Repeat the exercise, singing one of the tones.
5. Example 1.19 presents four-voice chords resulting from adding a tone to the triads above. Perform the same exercises as above, playing the chord with different structures of volume until the four join into one. Take note of the relative volume of the four individual tones.
6. Repeat the exercise, singing one of the tones.

Example 1.19.

Score Study

How we study a score depends on the goal of our performance. If the goal is to ensure the requisite performance as determined by the text, we ask: "*What does the score require?* What is the prescribed succession of tones, in what rhythms, at what volume, at what metronomic speed?" Studying then is essentially an act of memorization, with a questionable goal, as it is possible to realize a masterful score to the letter and produce a performance of limited aesthetic merit. If the goal is to visit our own unifying interpretation on an ensemble of musicians with divergent musical sensibilities and instincts, we ask: "*What do I require?* What happens, and how would I like it to sound? What's my interpretation?" That is an act of both memorization and self-indulgence, also quite possibly leading to a performance of limited aesthetic merit.

But if the goal is to produce the most moving, most exalting, most beautiful experience—as presumably was the composer's intent—then we ask: "*What do the sounds require?* How can these tones join together into a larger, singular whole?" In terms of the succession of tones, then, specifically: "What is the hierarchical dynamic structure within which I can unfold these tones such that they will lead to a singular experience?"

Studying the succession that is an entire movement involves precisely the same process as the dynamic analysis of a phrase described above: a two-part process at multiple levels. To reiterate, step 1 is determining where the groupings begin and end. A grouping consists of some creation of energy and some release; it begins with the creation of energy and ends when the next grouping begins—that is, with the next creation of energy. Step 2 is determining where the height of the energy must come so it is not fully dissipated before the grouping ends. The process extends up to and including the highest level of the hierarchy, the entire movement.

Because the grouping is a given, finding the dynamic structure of the entire movement involves only step 2, determining the height of the energy. In tonal works the primary driver of energy at the global level is the structural harmonic activity: specifically, the succession of fifth tonicizations away from the home key. The climax of the movement will come on the way to, within, or on the way out of the farthest key reached by successive fifth tonicizations away from the home key.[9]

Keep in mind that performers create the structure of energy using volume and rhythmic density. We create the dynamic structure at lower levels of the hierarchy largely with inflections of volume. On the global level of the entire movement, we create the dynamic structure with rhythmic density, increasing it by orienting the tempo forward toward the climax and decreasing it by orienting the tempo backward away from the climax. Keep in mind, too, that the more extensive the grouping, the more energy is required to sustain it; conversely, the shorter the grouping, the less energy is required. So a shorter phrase would tend to require less of an inflection of volume than a longer one, and a shorter movement would tend to require less of an increase in rhythmic density than a longer one.[10]

Studying in this way, we do not *memorize* the myriad individual tones; rather, in achieving an understanding of how the sounds can propel and sustain energy across the entire movement, we *learn* the whole work. Ultimately then, studying becomes largely a process of discovery, of uncovering the optimal structure of volume and temporality within which to unfold the work.

---

9   See the extensive discussion of tonicization in Thakar, *"Harp" Quartet*, particularly chapters 7 and 8.
10   See ibid., chapter 8, for an extended discussion of the use of volume and rhythmic density in creating the hierarchical dynamic structure.

Individuality

The obvious and important question arises: if the optimal dynamic structure and the optimal balance are givens—if they are elements of the composition—how do performers maintain individuality? In fact, no two
optimally beautiful performances could possibly be alike. Just as there
is a range of frequencies within which we can perceive an interval as in
tune and a range of tempos that we perceive as effective, there is a range of
optimal articulations, dynamic inflections, sound colors, and so on, all of
which will necessarily vary from performer to performer and from optimal
performance to optimal performance.

But more important, the goal of a performance is not, for most performers and listeners, to be different from other performances; it is to bring the
tones to life in a way that allows the most beautiful, most moving experience.[11]

Summary

In summary, our primary obligation as conductors is to empower the
ensemble to *make beautiful music*. This means coming to the podium
with an understanding of how the tones can come to life to allow the
most engaging, beautiful, transcendent experience, which depends on

---

[11] A performance certainly could emphasize inner voices of lesser consequence for the sake of individuality, or it could offer counterintuitive, inorganic inflections; such a performance may well be interesting intellectually. In fact, it is a common notion, especially among writers on music, that the value of
a performance lies in its difference from other performances . . . in its potential to reveal interesting
and previously unnoticed elements of the composition. But if Friday's performance is valuable to the
extent that it differs from Thursday's, then Saturday's performance must be different from the first two
to have value, and Sunday's must be a fourth way, and Monday's a fifth way, and so on. To dodge this
obvious absurdity—while maintaining that the value of a performance lies in its uniqueness—these
writers turn to qualifiers. Meyer, *Explaining Music*, and Schachter, "20th-Century Analysis," hold that
the performance must still be "convincing"; Cone, *Musical Form and Musical Performance*, maintains
that it must also be "valid" and "effective"; and Rink, "Analysis and (or?) Performance," requires it to
be "musically cogent." For Stein, *Form and Performance*, it cannot be "faulty"; for Dunsby, "Guest
Editorial," it cannot have "cheap theatrical tricks"; and for Berry, *Musical Structure and Performance*, it
must not contain "exaggerated, gratuitous effects." Unfortunately, these writers fail to address the one
critical question: *on what basis* is a performance convincing, valid, effective, or cogent; *on what basis* is
an element of that performance exaggerated, gratuitous, or a cheap theatrical trick? To be sure, there is
nothing wrong with listening to a performance to gain an enriched awareness of the varied and interesting elements of the composition. But it is also far from the most rewarding experience available.
Even one fiercely committed to a goal of intellectual enrichment eventually comes up against the fact
that the determinant of acceptability (validity, effectiveness, cogency) or unacceptability (faultiness,
exaggeration, theatricality) depends on the degree to which the performance allows a singular experience. In other words, it depends on the experience of beauty.

the tones joining together into a larger whole. We start with two essential parts of that understanding: structure of energy and balance. We can use our principal tools of volume and rhythmic density to create and release energy in order to achieve oneness of the entire hierarchical succession of tones of the movement, and we can also prioritize simultaneously sounding tones using volume to achieve a singular, compound sound in which all tones participate.

CHAPTER TWO

FREE THE MIND,
HEAR EVERYTHING

Connecting the Open Consciousness
to All the Sounds, All the Time

Optimally, the conductor's attentive consciousness is focused on the sounds: all the sounds, all the time. This means allowing all the sounds occurring at a given moment to register fully in the consciousness. And it means maintaining the entire continuum of sounds of the entire movement in the same conscious act; in other words, opening the consciousness to allow the already sounded tones and the tones not yet sounded to give meaning to the presently experienced ones. In short, the conductor is most effective who can *free the mind* from thoughts of any kind extraneous to the sounds and, with a freed mind, *hear everything*.

Tempo

Our ability to hear everything—to encompass all the simultaneously sounding tones as well as the entire continuum of sounded tones in a single act of consciousness—is very much affected by the tempo. Tempo, not the speed but the *quality of motion*, is an essential condition under which we experience the sounds. The quality (essential nature) of the motion is a function of the quantity of information processed in a given amount of time: the more information, the faster the quality of motion; the less information, the slower the quality of motion.

Note that tempo is closely related to—but fundamentally different from—speed. Speed is a quantifiable element of the physical world; tempo—quality of motion—is perceived. Consider riding a bicycle at thirty-five miles per hour over a bumpy road and driving a luxury car with the windows closed at sixty-five miles per hour on a highway. The bike ride is quantifiably slower than the drive, yet it feels faster. Consider a passage performed softly by a string quartet outdoors at a speed of seventy-two quarter notes per minute and the same passage played forcefully by a trombone choir in a small, resonant room at sixty-nine quarter notes per minute. The sounds from the string quartet dissipate; they are not loud to begin with, and they strike our ears a limited number of times as the sound waves continue out with limited or no reflection. The louder sounds from the trombones reach our ears numerous times as they bounce back and forth off the walls. The former is quantifiably faster, but because it presents less information in a similar span of time we experience it as slower. Because all we have is our experience, the quality of the motion—the essential nature of the motion—is slower, and thus the tempo is slower. In such a case, faster speed, slower tempo.

There is no precisely correct tempo, but there are wrong tempos. A wrong tempo prevents the tones from being absorbed in a single act of consciousness. A tempo is too fast if we are unable to perceive each and every sound fully—if there is insufficient time for each tone to register wholly in the consciousness. In a too-fast tempo the tones are blurred or incomplete, they lose their individuality and along with it their capacity to give meaning to the other tones, and thus they cannot join together in a single act of consciousness.

A tempo is too slow if we are unable to maintain the entire continuum of tones in a single act of consciousness, in other words, in a single extended present. Imagine hearing a word, for example the word RUN.[1] The word has three component phonemes, R, U, and N. Each phoneme is given meaning by earlier phonemes that participate in the same singular object of consciousness. When we hear the N, the R and U have already passed, yet they continue to be part of our consciousness during the sounding of the N. The R and U give meaning to the N because they remain part of a singular, present consciousness of the entire word. In the word SUN, for example, the N phoneme is the same as in RUN, but it is given a different meaning by changing the R to S.

---

[1] See also Thakar, *"Harp" Quartet*, chapter 1.

Each phoneme is given meaning not only by previous phonemes but also by the phonemes yet to come. When we hear the R of Run, the U and N have yet to sound, but they give meaning to the R because they participate in a singular consciousness of the entire word. For example, the R would have a different meaning in the words Rug or Ran. The R phoneme is the same, but its meaning depends on the phonemes to come within the same object of a singular, present consciousness. And, of course, when we hear the U of Run, it is given meaning by its participation in a single extended present consciousness that includes the previously sounded R and the yet-to-come N.

This same phenomenon takes place on multiple levels. Consider the sentence "I run to the store." During my consciousness of each new word, each of the previous words is retained, so that during the sounding of the word "store," the words "I run to the" are retained in the same present consciousness. If the sentence were changed to "You run to the store," the words following the "You" would take on a different meaning, but only if the first word was maintained in present consciousness during the entire sentence. Words are also given meaning by words yet to come. If the original sentence was "I run the store," the meaning of the word "run" is fundamentally changed by the words that follow it, but only if the words yet to come are part of present consciousness during the word "run."

Music works in a similar way. Tones in a succession have meaning given by the preceding tones, but only if those preceding tones are retained in the same present consciousness. And currently sounding tones are also given meaning by the tones as yet to come, but only if they too join all the tones in a single act of consciousness. A too-slow musical tempo precludes us from maintaining all the tones—the previously sounded tones and the yet-to-come tones—in the same present consciousness and thus prevents the tones from giving meaning to each other within the larger whole.

Finding the tempo for a musical performance is comparable to finding the distance from which to view a painting. When I approach a painting in a museum, the first thing I do is walk toward it and away from it, to find a point from which I can perceive the entire painting and only the painting. Standing too close to the painting, I cannot keep all the components in my consciousness simultaneously; this is equivalent to a too-slow tempo. Standing too far from the painting, I cannot fully perceive the individual component shapes, which blur together; this is equivalent to a too-fast tempo. Given a great painting, there is a range of distance from which

I can fully perceive all the individual components simultaneously.[2] And given a masterwork composition, there is a range of tempo within which I can fully perceive all the individual components simultaneously—that is, within the same singular act of consciousness.

To repeat, the tempo—or quality of motion—is a function of how much information we have to process: the more information, the faster the quality of motion; the less information, the slower the quality of motion. Tempo is affected by multiple factors. Speed is by far the most determinative: the faster we play, the more information we have to process and thus the faster the quality of motion. But other factors affect the amount of information we receive and thus impact the quality of motion. A larger ensemble, a higher volume, a greater degree of inflections, and a more resonant room would all increase the amount of information that reaches the ear. Additional factors include register (lower tones provide more information than higher ones because they have more overtones within the range of hearing), articulations (longer tones provide more information than shorter ones), and sound quality (richer tones provide more information than more transparent ones).

ESSENTIAL PRINCIPLE: Finding the Tempo

Finding an effective tempo is a critical responsibility of the performer—arguably the most critical. At essence it involves two simple conditions: (1) it must be slow enough that each tone can register fully in the consciousness, and (2) it must be fast enough that the entire continuum of tones can be maintained in the same act of consciousness. In other words, it comes down to *hearing everything* in two ways: (1) hearing every sounding tone, and (2) hearing the entire succession of tones at the same time. If each individual tone works fully on your consciousness, and if you maintain in consciousness the first tone while you hear the second, and the first and second while you hear the third, and so on and so forth through the entire movement, you will have found a perfectly effective tempo.

---

[2]   It is surprising and disappointing that many museum curators do not understand this essential point, as paintings stacked one on top of another, displayed in a narrow hallway, or hung far above normal eye level cannot provide the viewer with an optimal experience of beauty.

PRACTICAL MATTER: Tempo Direction
Referring to a Specific Note Value

Although finding a tempo depends entirely on the two conditions outlined above, it can help to consider the note value to which the tempo directions refer. For example, when Mozart describes the tempo of the second movement of his Symphony no. 40 as Andante, the "walking" characteristic is given by the eighth note, not the dotted quarter note. In the third movement of Mendelssohn's Symphony no. 3 it is the quarter note he describes as Adagio, not the eighth note; similarly, in the opening of *La Mer* Debussy describes the dotted half note, not the quarter note, as Très lent. And in the third movement of his Symphony no. 9, Beethoven describes the quarter note as first Molto vivace and then—after a stringendo—as Presto.[3]

A word about metronome markings: if the composer specifies a metronome marking, is this not a hard and fast direction, like pitches and rhythms? Are we not obligated to observe it? The simple answer is . . . no. Metronome markings can at best guide a performer to an effective tempo range, but they are largely irrelevant.

Most of what is marked in a score is in fact approximate. For example, pitch indications for all variable-pitched instruments are approximate. A range of frequencies can be heard as, say, B♭, and the composer expects the musician to choose the one that allows that B♭ to join with the other tones. Rhythms are also approximate: there is a range of temporal placements

---

[3] Confusion as to the tempo relations in this movement results from Beethoven's metronome markings: whole note = 116 for the Molto vivace and then, following a stringendo to Presto, half note (!) = 116. This marking would result in a bar of the Presto half the speed of a bar of the Molto vivace: one bar at 116 to one bar at 58. At a speed of whole note = 58, that music could not possibly be understood as Presto; perhaps we would describe it is as Andante or Andante quasi Allegretto. Nobody, not even the most ardent literalist, takes a bar of the Presto at half the speed of the Molto vivace. The only logical assumption is that Beethoven—severely mathematically challenged—made a mistake by writing half note = 116 instead of whole note = 116; in other words, he intended a temporal equality of the bar in both sections, with the three quarter notes per bar Molto vivace (116) moving via a stringendo to a Presto with four notes to the same bar (also at 116). This also makes musical sense, as it allows the climax to come within the Presto section. The traditional solution, however, is odd and difficult to understand. The Presto is traditionally played faster than whole note = 58 but at a perfectly moderate pace, something like whole note = 72. According to Celibidache (Munich Philharmonic *Dirigierskurs*, 1981), if the movement were a house it would fall down. And famously per Mahler, "Tradition ist Schlamperei."

within which, say, three tones can be heard as an eighth note and two sixteenth notes. The composer expects the musician to choose the particular temporal location of the tones—perhaps settled on the back of the beat, or moving forward, or "cheating" the sixteenth notes, or precisely rhythmic—that allows these tones to join with all the others into a larger organic whole. The same is true of dynamic and articulation markings.

Metronome markings are the only precisely measurable indication in a score, but they simply indicate speed. We do not experience the speed, we experience the quality of motion, which results from a number of factors. Depending on the amount of sound information—hall resonance, number of instruments, degree of inflections—the metronomic speed indicated might result in an effective tempo, or a too-fast one or a too-slow one.

Some metronome markings could never result in an effective tempo. Note recorded performances conducted by the composer—notably Stravinsky, Copland, and Elgar—that are dramatically at variance with their own metronome markings. And consider Beethoven's metronome markings, widely held to result in too-fast performances; they were not created until 1817, by which time Beethoven was virtually completely deaf.[4]

The conductor who hears the tones unfolding as one—allowing all the tones to register and maintaining the entire continuum of tones in the attentive consciousness—will settle on a speed that results in an effective tempo. But because tempo is determined by multiple factors beyond speed, the conductor who does not hear the tones unfolding as one will likely not find an effective tempo even at the same precise metronome mark. Ultimately, slavish observance of a metronome mark is the product of a lazy or dull mind and the sign of a limited musician.[5]

PRACTICAL MATTER: Rhythm and Tempo

In finding an effective tempo it is critical to have an impeccable connection to the rhythm, in particular to the internal divisions of every beat. While the metronome may not determine an effective tempo, the machine itself is not without value. In developing an impeccable sense of rhythm it can be helpful to use a metronome during the study process, ticking not just the beats but the internal divisions.

---

[4] An appropriate speed for imagined sounds tends to be faster than one for sounds actually experienced.

[5] Sergiu Celibidache (Munich Philharmonic *Dirigierskurs*): "The day I learn something about music from a metronome is the day I will study with one."

EXERCISE: Touching the Sounds

There are no sounds in the physical world; there are only compressions and rarefactions of air molecules, which become translated into sounds in our brains. Nonetheless, we perceive the sounds as being "out there," existing in space. In hearing all the sounds as you conduct, be sure you are physically open to them; even feel as though you are touching them, surrounding them.

With a recording, preferably playing on speakers, close your eyes, and make sure that every sound registers fully on your consciousness. Imagine that the sounds have actual physical properties, sense the sounds in the space they occupy in front of you, and encircle them with open arms. Louder sounds with more expansive registers will seem to occupy a larger space; softer sounds within a limited register will seem to occupy a smaller space. The exercise would be particularly effective if performed with an ensemble of live musicians, although opportunities to do so are clearly rare.

EXERCISES: Finding the Tempo

1. The best way to gain proficiency in finding a tempo is to listen intently to live performances, for the express purpose of connecting with the tempo.[6] Allow all the sounds occurring in succession to register fully in your consciousness, and try to maintain all those sounds in the same act of consciousness. (It may help to do this with eyes closed.) If the former is not possible, the tempo is likely too fast; if the latter is not possible, the tempo is likely too slow. But if you are able to do both, the performers have found an effective tempo.

2. Ask a group to perform a passage too fast—so that each tone does not have its full appropriate temporal space. Then ask the group to perform it too slowly—so that it is not possible to retain all the tones in the focused consciousness. Finally, ask them to play at an effective tempo, not too fast or too slow.

---

[6] Recordings would not be helpful for determining effective tempos, as the information available from a recording is essentially different from that of the original live performance. This is due in part to the loss of sound information as it travels in multiple steps from the concert hall to the room speakers, in part to compression of the sound (reduction of the high and low frequencies), and in part to the fact that the acoustic of the room into which the sound waves flow from the speakers is different from that of the original hall in which the live sound was produced.

Trust

An essential component of the process of music making as a conductor is trust. Focusing on the sounds to the exclusion of all else—giving oneself over completely to the sounds—cannot happen without trust, both of yourself and of the musicians.

Trust your own musicianship, trust that all you need to do is absorb sound and respond. You do not need to prove anything, and you do not need to demonstrate individuality; these require the focused attention on matters external to the sounds. And you can have confidence; you can trust your response. All humans have a capacity to respond to and be moved by sounds similarly; surely your open response to sounds is not inadequate. As your musicianship is all you have, you have nothing to lose by trusting yourself.

And you must trust the musicians in your care. If you do not trust them, your function is limited to ensuring when and how they play, which fundamentally changes your conscious focus away from absorbing the sounds. Musicians with a conductor whose responsibility is limited to ensuring when and how they play are similarly limited: their principal responsibility becomes responding to the conductor instead of to the sounds, very much to the detriment of their ability to make music at the highest level.

ESSENTIAL PRINCIPLE:
Conduct the Sounds, Not the Musicians

Trust yourself and trust the musicians to respond to the demands of the sounds; conduct the sounds, not the musicians; guide the musicians to those sounds by responding to the sounds yourself. In short, meet the musicians at the sounds.

Rehearsing

In the words of the legendary conductor Sergiu Celibidache, we rehearse like a sculptor sculpts, not like a painter paints.[7] A painter begins with a blank canvas and adds material until the truth—maximal beauty—is achieved. A sculptor starts with a block of material and removes the conditions that stand in the way of the truth, until the truth is revealed. So too we rehearse: "No, too loud; no, too late; no, too sharp; no; no; no. . . . . Yes!"

Hearing everything, then, is critical to the rehearsal process, which involves three essential questions: (1) Is it magical . . . is it transcendent, moving? (2) If not, why not? and (3) What's the remedy? If the sounds do not allow for a transcendent experience, we identify the offending condition(s): pitch, ensemble, balance, phrasing inflection, sound quality, and so on—and offer a solution with respect and diplomacy. But the process must begin with the conductor open to all the sounds—hearing everything—and open to the possibility of being moved by them.

> ### EXERCISE: Attend Rehearsals Attentively
>
> Outside of rehearsing chamber music as a performer, the best way to learn about rehearsing is to attend rehearsals attentively. Listen intently. Does it move you? No? Why not? How would you fix it? Did the conductor hear the same problem, and did it get fixed? How? Or did the conductor stop for something you didn't hear? Was that fixed? If so, how, and was it better? A great deal can be learned about rehearsing from attending rehearsals aggressively, both good and bad rehearsals.

Conducting without a Score

To paraphrase Stanisław Skrowaczewski, "If using a score is distracting, don't; if not using one is more distracting, do."[8]

A masterwork is a masterwork because it allows its unfolding as a logical, organic whole, one in which elements follow in succession as a matter of necessity. The conductor's highest responsibility is to come to the podium with an understanding of that possibility.

---

7   Celibidache during the Munich Philharmonic *Dirigierskurs.*
8   Skrowaczewski, Colorado Symphony Orchestra post-concert lecture, Denver, 1995.

For the conductor with such an understanding, the object of conscious-ness can be the totality of the sounds in a given movement, from beginning to end, all in the same act of consciousness. No score is necessary.

Not only is a score unnecessary for that conductor, but it would be a significant distraction. The primary object of consciousness would become the relationship of the sounds to the score rather than the relationship of the sounds to themselves. And in the act of turning pages, the object of the focused consciousness is that very act. While conducting with a score may well offer an experience of beauty (there is beauty on all levels), it precludes an unfettered immersion in the sounds.

If, on the other hand, the work does not allow its unfolding as an organic whole, if the tones do not unfold inevitably, then conducting with-out a score is a matter of memorization. The object of my conscious act in conducting a succession of tones I have memorized is "What comes next?" This too is a distraction.

The decision of whether to use a score rests on which you find more distracting. Conducting without a score usually involves some degree of memorization, as only a handful of the most profound masterworks allow their unfolding as a singular whole, and every work worth per-forming will have some discernible potential for singularity. If in a given movement the inevitable unfolding of the sounds outweighs the con-scious focus on "what comes next," the exalting experience available is worth not using a score. If, however, the necessity of focusing on "what comes next" is sufficiently distracting from experiencing the sounds, then it is advisable to use a score. Although conducting without a score may seem daunting, invariably people find it easier and more rewarding than imagined. And coming to the podium without a score requires a greater understanding of how the work unfolds. So in short: if the work allows it, conduct without a score.

PRACTICAL MATTER: Hearing Everything

Study so that you can hear all the sounds internally, in your "mind's ear," without a score. People learn in different ways and bring different skills and aptitudes to the process. I recommend a multi-faceted approach, beginning with simply opening the score and hearing it.[9]

It is helpful to hear at pitch, so you might want a keyboard handy to ensure that you stay on pitch in your imaginary hearing. Once you have a grasp of the melodies and harmonies of a movement, try standing and conducting through it, gradually adding to your understanding of the totality of the instruments.

Recordings can be extremely helpful, too, not to copy any element of that performance but simply to confirm your sense of the ensemble sound. Listen carefully—repeatedly if necessary—until you are sure you are allowing all the tones to register with you.

Summary

Hearing everything—allowing all the concurrently sounding tones and the entire continuum of those tones to register in the consciousness—is a fundamental requisite for a conductor to make music at the highest level. Hearing everything is critical to finding the tempo, because a performance led by a conductor who allows all the tones to register fully will not—cannot—be too fast, and a performance led by a conductor who maintains all the tones in a single act of consciousness will not—cannot—be too slow. Hearing everything requires a mind freed from everything external to the sounds. And it requires trust in the musicians and trust in oneself to let go of everything outside of those sounds.

---

[9]   This is an essential skill. To some it comes easily; others can develop it with slow, careful work. One recommended approach is to use Bach chorales, singing each tone of a chord up from the bass, then singing the next chord and repeating the process until the sound of the harmony becomes ingrained. Then add a third chord, and a fourth, and so on. Finally, play a phrase of the chorale singing one line—perhaps the bass line—and go as slowly as necessary to be able to hear the next harmony before you perform it. Keyboard harmony exercises, even for non-keyboard players, can also be extremely helpful—again performing them as slowly as necessary to hear the next harmony before it sounds.

CHAPTER THREE

FREE THE BODY

Involving the Necessity of Freeing the Body from Unnecessary Muscle Tensions

Conducting technique is the ability to influence sounds using physical gestures. Physical gestures can influence sounds to the extent that they conform to those sounds; conversely, gestures that conflict with the sounds have limited influence. Conforming gestures to sounds requires efficient use of the muscles—in other words, using only the muscles necessary. Thus, the most critical element of developing conducting technique is learning to *free the body* from unnecessary muscle tensions.

Why a Conductor?

Why do we need a conductor? How is it that duos, trios, quartets, quintets, and so on, all can make music superbly without one?

At its very essence, music making is about the coming together of many into one: of many tones into a singular object and of many musicians into a unified ensemble. Coming together—interpersonal synchronicity—is an essential human instinct. Consider couples whose breathing and heart rates become synchronized, or congregational recitations, in which invariably the congregants join quickly into a relatively unified rhythm.[1]

---

[1] See three studies of interpersonal synchronicity: Helm, Sbarra, and Ferrer, "Assessing Cross-Partner Associations in Physiological Responses"; Ferrer and Helm, "Dynamical Systems Modeling of Physiological Coregulation in Dyadic Interactions"; Miyake, "Co-creation Systems: Ma and Communication."

We are able to come together because—while each of us is a product of a different set of experiences, all of which inform our perceptions and responses—*human beings respond to stimuli in the same or similar ways.* For example, normal human beings perceive a red traffic light and respond by stopping.[2] My perception of the red light is assuredly not your perception; they are two different, separate acts of consciousness. But in each of our independent acts of consciousness, the object of our consciousness is the same: we both perceive the red light, and further, both of our perceptions of it come with the assumption that the other has the same perception. In fact the light works as a signal to stop only because of this essentially similar human response.

Musicians respond to the stimuli of sounds. Assuming the musicians of an ensemble are open to the sounds, they respond to those sounds in the same or similar ways.[3] Chamber musicians are constantly adjusting to the sounds: to intonation, to meter (ensemble), to articulations, to timbre, and to energy. For example, a chamber musician makes a crescendo, building energy. The other musicians hear that crescendo and relax the tempo sufficiently to play out that extra energy; in other words, they respond to the demands of the sounds. And they respond on multiple levels: for example, they play together in relaxing the tempo not only because each responds to the necessity of that relaxation in a similar way but because they respond to and join the collective slowing pulse.

Visual Confirmation

Musicians in the act of playing respond physically to the sounds, conforming motions of their body to the pulse and character. Chamber musicians' primary means of connecting to each other is through hearing, but they have the added benefit of visual confirmation. Visual perception of the physical movements of their colleagues *confirms* the musicians' essential responsibility of coming together through responding to the demands of the sounds.[4] Or, more simply: hearing determines, seeing confirms.

---

[2] People who are colorblind, as is my son, may not perceive the light as red; colorblindness is an abnormality.

[3] Of course, this is not true of musicians who—in hearing sounds—focus attention on a nonmusical object, such as a frightening audition experience with the passage, or a glorious previous performance, or the teacher with whom they studied, and so on. These are objects of consciousness that clearly differ from person to person.

[4] In fact, a common rehearsal technique for chamber ensembles is to force themselves to hear each other by turning their chairs back-to-back, eliminating the "crutch" of visual contact.

Musicians in larger ensembles also make music on the basis of hearing. If the ensemble is too large for each musician to have visual contact with every other, a conductor is useful. Each musician can then have visual contact with the conductor, who uses physical gestures to confirm musicians' aural connections to the sounds. Synchronized with the sounds in every respect possible, the conductor's physical motions become the guide that helps connect the musicians to each other and to the sounds.

But the conductor does more than simply provide visual confirmation. Just as musicians incorporate the physical motions of other musicians in their response to the sounds, they also incorporate the physical motions of the conductor in their response. The conductor participates in the music making fully, albeit silently. And as the only person onstage who has visual contact with every musician, the conductor becomes *the most influential musician.*

Required to make music using only the body, the conductor is in a uniquely disadvantageous position. But the conductor is also in a uniquely advantageous position. Freed from the necessity of focusing the attentive consciousness on the playing of an instrument, freed from the physical restrictions involved in playing that instrument, and centrally located to all the sounds, the conductor can devote an unencumbered consciousness and an unencumbered body to the totality of the sounds.[5]

Alignment and Balance

Essential to a conductor's effectiveness as a physical manifestation of the sounds is an optimal physical foundation, both for what we communicate to the musicians and for what we receive. Although it may seem trivial, our physical foundation—the alignment and balance of our bones—informs every element of our ability to fulfill our responsibilities.

Any use of the body—standing, walking, gesturing—involves the musculoskeletal system: muscles acting on bones. Muscles work in one way: they tense, or contract. To conform our gestures to sounds requires us to contract specific muscles in specific ways, and of course we can use these muscles only when they are available—in other words, when they are not otherwise contracted.

Freedom of the muscles begins with the alignment and balance of the bones. Consider the human skeleton: bones of the feet support the leg

---

[5] The conductor has an additional advantage in focusing on the totality of the sounds in that the preparation process begins with a score encompassing all the parts.

bones, which support the pelvis, which supports the spine, which supports the ribs and the bones of the shoulders and arms, on top of which rests the head. Such a flimsy structure cannot stand of its own accord.

Fortunately, our bodies are "structures magnificently capable of withstanding the pressures of life on this planet."[6] One of those pressures is the force of gravity, so we have a system of muscles to stabilize us. To keep us standing erect, the brain sends a message for stabilizing muscles to contract, steadying the joints.[7] With the bones in alignment, each from the bottom up optimally balanced, only normal, minimal stabilizing muscle tensions are needed. With bones out of alignment, however, additional muscles are put to work. For example, as you bend forward, the calf muscles contract and stiffen to prevent you from falling. As you lean to one side, abdominal muscles on the opposite side contract and stiffen.

Unfortunately, many of us reach maturity accustomed to carrying our bones out of alignment. We slouch, we lean, we tilt our heads, we elevate one or both shoulders, and so on, all of which necessitates compensatory and detrimental muscular tension. To achieve a position of alignment and balance requires not only learning how to use the body; it also requires the much more difficult *unlearning* of processes ingrained from years of misuse.

EXERCISE: Alignment and Balance

With feet equidistant and facing forward, feel the weight of your body balanced between your heels and the balls of your feet. Rotate the pelvis, sensing the changing of the balancing muscle tension in your legs, until you feel them aligned over your feet, with minimal tension in the leg muscles. Rotate the shoulders over your pelvis, sensing the changing of the balancing muscle tension in the abdominal muscles, until you feel them aligned, with minimal tension. Similarly rotate your head, sensing the changing of the balancing muscle tension in the neck, until you feel it aligned, with minimal tension. It may help to note that the head rests on the spine approximately midway between the ears, which is considerably higher than most of us intuit.

---

[6] Stephen Bender, DC, email to the author, July 20, 2015.

[7] More precisely, standing is not a position of stasis: the brain monitors the constantly shifting conditions—of body orientation, of weight redistribution, of wind, and so on—and initiates the appropriate constant adjustments in the stabilizing muscles and the fascia (the continuous system of connective tissue that gives muscle shape).

Taking a page from Alexander Technique, now direct your head forward and up. Keeping conscious of how your head connects to the spine, allow the spine to lengthen and the back to widen, with shoulders oriented outward. When you achieve an optimal alignment and associated muscular freedom, you may well feel a sense of lightness, as if your body is floating, suspended from your head.

You may also find value in using a balance board, and purposefully moving in and out of balance, to develop the key skill of returning to a position of alignment and balance.[8]

NB. Conductors with significant alignment problems are well advised to do regular and committed work with one of the many strategies for achieving body alignment, such as Alexander Technique, yoga, chiropractic, massage therapy, Pilates, Feldenkrais, or tai chi.

Muscles

Aside from stabilizing joints, the other primary function of the skeletal muscles is to move bones. In broad terms, to move a bone, muscles attached to that bone and another bone contract, reducing the distance between the two attach points and pulling the bones closer together. To move that same bone in the opposite direction, other muscles attached to the opposite side of the bones contract, reducing the distance between the attach points on that side and expanding the distance between the bones.[9]

Muscle tension that reduces the distance between a bone and another bone closer to the center of the body is flexion. For example, to make a fist, we flex the fingers by contracting flexor muscles on the inside (palm side) of the hand; these muscles are attached to the fingers at one end and the forearm and upper arm at the other. Muscle tension that increases the distance between a bone and another bone closer to the center of the body is extension. To straighten the fingers out of the fist, we release the flexor muscles and contract extensor muscles on the outside of the hand (the

---

8   An effective balance board can be constructed easily by centering a 4″ × 4″ × 2″ block of wood on the bottom of a 2′ × 2′ × ⅝″ plywood board.

9   For a visual representation of the muscles at work, I recommend a remarkable resource: the computer program Muscle Premium by *Visible Body*, www.visiblebody.com.

fingernail side), attached to the fingers at one end and the forearm and upper arm at the other.

It is the rare person who reaches maturity moving with complete efficiency, using only the muscles necessary. Unnecessary tensions in the muscles of the arms, shoulders, and chest are common, and they prevent gestures from conforming fully to the sounds. Also common and detrimental are unnecessary tensions in the muscles of the neck, legs, jaw, forehead, and hand (particularly the baton hand).

Freeing the Arms

The essence of a well-formed beat gesture is an ascent and descent of the hand perpendicular to the ground using only the muscles necessary. The motion involves flexion of the upper arm at the shoulder (rotating the upper arm forward in the shoulder socket) as well as a slight flexion and then extension of the forearm at the elbow (decreasing and increasing the angle of the forearm and upper arm). Lowering the hand back to the lowest point is accomplished by the release of those muscles.[10]

Few adults perform this simple action of raising the hand with complete efficiency. It is common to add unnecessary tensions while raising the arms, primarily by abducting the upper arm (bringing the elbows out to the sides), by elevating (shrugging) the shoulders, and by contracting the pectoral muscles of the chest.[11] While it may seem trivial, tension in these muscles significantly limits our ability to fully conform gesture to sound. Thus, learning to raise the arms perpendicular to the ground without tensing these muscles is essential to developing full physical control—in other words, without raising the elbows to the sides or elevating the shoulders.

---

[10] The only muscles necessary to flex the shoulder (raising the upper arm forward) are the two heads of the biceps and the anterior deltoid muscles that attach at the bones of the shoulder girdle and the forearm, and the coracobrachialis muscle that attaches at the bones of the shoulder girdle and the upper arm, with some assistance from the pectoral muscle of the chest. The muscles necessary to flex the forearm at the elbow are the biceps, plus the brachialis and brachioradialis muscles that attach at the upper arm and the bones of the forearm.

[11] Abducting the upper arm is accomplished by contracting the medial or middle part of the deltoid. The deltoid is the large, thick, three-part muscle that covers the shoulder. All three parts of the deltoid attach to the upper arm and the shoulder girdle (collarbone and shoulder blade). Tensing the posterior (rear) deltoid raises the upper arm to the rear; this is a muscle we use only when the descent of the arm must be faster than gravity can accomplish. Tensing the anterior (front) deltoid assists in raising the upper arm forward. Elevating the shoulders is accomplished by contracting the trapezius muscles, the large flat muscles that cover and control the back of the shoulder blade and neck, and the levator scapulae, which attach at the side of the neck. In elevating the shoulders, some add unnecessary tension in the anterior deltoid and in the pectoral muscles of the chest.

EXERCISE: Basic Position

The first step in freeing the arms from unnecessary tension is find-ing the *basic position*, the neutral position of least tension. Stand—with feet equidistant and facing forward, roughly shoulder-width apart—in optimal alignment, weight evenly distributed, head for-ward and up, spine lengthened, back widened. With palms facing inward to your sides, swing your arms freely backward and forward, stopping when the forearms are roughly parallel with the floor at the bottom of the conducting space. Then pronate the forearms, turning the palms to the ground.[12] The arms should be somewhat forward to allow for the use of the whole arm. Holding the arms too close to the body—creating, say, a 90° angle of the elbow joint—results in minimal upper arm rotation at the shoulder, thus limiting power. Extending the arms too far from the body—approaching a straight line between upper arm and forearm—results in restricted motion of the forearm at the elbow, thus limiting flexibility. It may help to think of having the elbows forward from the center of the body or to think an angle of roughly 135° at the elbow.[13] The hands extend forward from the forearm, palms down, with the wrist not locked but supple. The fingers extend casually forward as well. See video demonstration 3.1 (available at www.markandthakar.com/OnConducting, as are subsequent video demonstrations).

To check yourself, shrug your shoulders forcefully, tensing the trapezius muscles; then slam your shoulders down, releasing the tension. And, keeping your hands in place, rotate your elbows until they find the lowest point. See video demonstration 3.2.

Working with a partner is highly recommended. With your arms in the basic position, have the partner take hold of your

---

[12] It is helpful to keep your palms to your sides with elbows pointing toward the back as you raise your arms into the basic position and then pronate the forearms. If the pronation occurs with the arms at your sides, it is easy to involve the entire arm including the upper arm, pointing the elbows out to your sides (medial rotation of the shoulders), which is accomplished by contracting the pectoralis major. Pronating the forearms only after raising them prevents this unnecessary and detrimental muscle tension. Note that pronation does require some tension in the pronator muscles of the forearm. These muscles are small, the resultant tension is minimal, and the benefit of allowing the wrist joint to move in concert with the arm far outweighs the cost in extra forearm tension. And especially in strong beats some may find half pronation more successful.

[13] This default position does require some tension in the anterior deltoid to flex the upper arm forward. To many—especially those with long arms—it may well seem uncomfortably far. The issue though is not how far forward the arms are, it is situating them to allow full use of the requisite arm muscles.

hands. Let all the tension out of your arm muscles so the arms are held up only by your partner. The partner should be able to feel the heaviness in your arms if all tension is gone. This can be checked by suddenly letting go: the arms will drop like dead weights only if all the tension is gone. With the partner holding your hands and with your arms completely free of tension, slowly add only enough tension so the arms do not fall, ultimately holding your arms up yourself with the least tension necessary. See video demonstration 3.3.

EXERCISE: Raising and Lowering the Arms

Start in the basic position. Keeping your arms and shoulders free, raise your hands to the full height of the conducting space, a bit higher than your head. It is important to keep the hands ascending straight up, perpendicular to the ground (although toward the top of an ascent to full height, the arm will arc slightly in toward the body). Freeze your arms in place when they reach the top. See video demonstration 3.4.

With a partner holding on to your hands, release all tension. Again, your partner can tell if you release all tension, as your arms will be heavy. If you have successfully raised your arms without unnecessary tension, your arms will maintain the same shape. However, if the arms or shoulders drop as you release all tension, then you added unnecessary tension on the way up. See video demonstration 3.5.

If your elbows dropped, then you tensed unnecessary muscles during the ascent, likely the medial deltoids. It can be helpful to identify the medial deltoid muscle tactilely. With your right arm in basic position, put your left hand on the outside of your right upper arm, near the shoulder, and rotate your elbow out to the side. You should feel the medial deltoid tensing and releasing. With the medial deltoid released, begin to raise your right hand perpendicular to the ground. Keep your left hand on the muscle to ensure that it remains free. Then repeat the process on the opposite side, with your right hand on your left arm. See video demonstration 3.6.

If your shoulders dropped, then you added tension in the trapezius or the upper pectoral muscles. To check the pectoral muscles, with your right arm in basic position, put your left hand on the right side of your chest, with your fingers touching roughly halfway between the nipple and the collarbone. Consciously tense and release the pectoral muscle. With the pectoral muscle released, begin to raise your right hand perpendicular to the ground. Keep your left hand on the muscle to ensure that it remains free. Repeat on the opposite side. See video demonstration 3.7.

To check the trapezius muscles, have a partner keep his or her hands on top of the shoulders, with one hand on either side of the neck. The trapezius muscles will move as the skeletal structures shift with the raising of your arms, but they should not tense, elevating the shoulder in a shrugging motion. See video demonstration 3.8.

Once you've identified the offending muscles and the point in the ascent at which you tense them, freeing them is a matter of mind over muscle. It is your brain informing your muscles to move, so it may help to monitor closely what your brain is telling your arms. From a basic position, first imagine that you are about to raise your arms, but don't raise them. Take careful note of what muscles begin to tense. Then think: "I'm not going to raise my arms; I'm simply going to allow them to float up."

It may help to think consciously of widening your back, understanding that the arm/shoulder mechanism actually begins where the collarbone meets the top of the breastbone. It may also help to think of raising your arms from the fingertips.

Try working in small segments of the ascent. For example, start halfway up, with a partner ensuring full freedom, as above. Let the arms descend ever so slowly, just a few inches, then ascend back to the starting position. Check for freedom of the muscles at each stopping point. Note that in any ascent of the arms perpendicular to the ground the shoulder always participates: the upper arm always rotates forward at the shoulder joint, even in the smallest motion. In this process it may help to feel that your arm hangs from your wrist, as if your wrist were held up by a string, and that the top of the wrist is leading the ascent. See video demonstration 3.9.

Of critical importance, though, is to understand that if you've been raising your arms using excess muscle tension for years, this is what will feel natural and free. With a partner holding your arms, if you release all tension and your arms drop further, then the muscles were assuredly not free! To repeat: vigilance in gaining complete freedom from unnecessary muscle tension is a critical first step in developing conducting technique, that is, the ability to conform gestures to sounds.

Lowering the arms is simply a matter of retracing the path of the ascent, returning to the basic position. Avoid locking the elbows on the descent, such that the arms retreat in toward the body. In other words, make sure your hands descend in the same vertical plane perpendicular to the ground, keeping the elbow joints flexible so the arms return to the basic position with elbows somewhat forward from the body. Further, take care that both elbow and wrist reach bottom at the same time or, more precisely, that the rotation around the shoulder and the opening of the elbow stop at the same time. As you feel the fingertips leading on the ascent, it may also help to feel the elbow leading on the descent.

You can practice on your own with the help of a bookshelf. Find a shelf at the height of your hands in the basic position, roughly at navel level. With your wrist on the shelf, free your arms so they are held up entirely by the shelf. Be extremely careful about freeing the arms, as it is easy to assume that the muscles are free, ignoring unnecessary muscle tensions you live with constantly. Slowly inject enough tension to hold them up yourself, and step back from the shelf. Now raise your hands to the level of a higher shelf, allowing them to float, staying vigilant about unnecessary tension. Step forward, place your wrists on the higher shelf, and release all tension, so that your arms are supported completely by the higher shelf. If your arms dropped, you added tension on the way up. Start over, working carefully until you can reach the higher shelf without any unnecessary tension—so that releasing tension does not change the shape of your arms.

Try also beginning the bookshelf exercise with the arms at the higher level. Lower them and raise them back to the higher level; then check for freedom from unnecessary tension.

Other Unnecessary Tensions

Neck and Head

Unnecessary tensions also commonly occur in the muscles of the neck, the jaw, and the forehead. The neck is manipulated by a series of muscles attached to the front and back of the occipital bone located at the bottom rear of the cranium. Clenching the jaw results from tensing a series of muscles on the sides of the head. Tightening the forehead muscles in a frowning gesture, which creates vertical creases at the bottom center of the forehead, results from tensing muscles at the top of the nose and above the eyes. All of these unnecessary tensions restrict the free connection of physical motions to sounds.

EXERCISES: Neck and Head

To overcome the habit of tensing the neck muscles, practice conducting while rotating your head around your neck slowly in a full circle, going as far forward, backward, and to either side as possible. Note that the neck actually begins between the ears, where the spine meets the head. To overcome the habit of tensing the jaw muscles, practice conducting open-mouthed, with the jaw fully depressed. To overcome the habit of tensing the forehead muscles in a frown, practice conducting with raised eyebrows, which results in horizontal creases in the forehead.

Reminder: in releasing any unnecessary tensions, it can help to think about making the gesture in question without actually making it, taking note of the muscles that begin to tense unnecessarily. Then make the gesture, allowing the body to move as if of its own accord—in other words, without the unnecessary and debilitating tension. And keep in mind again that lengthening the spine and allowing your body to float from the head requires freedom from unnecessary tension in the neck and head muscles.

Hand (Wrist and Fingers)

The hand extends out from the forearm, palm down, and the fingers are extended casually. Keep in mind that the bones of the hand and fingers actually begin at the wrist. The wrist joint is supple, with the flexibility to rise as the arm rises (in other words, to lift the hand at the wrist above the level of the forearm).[14] As a rule, the hand should not descend below the level of the forearm. Particularly critical is that the hand not work in opposition to the arm—in other words, that the hand not continue descending below the level of the forearm as the arm has begun ascending. This "flopping" motion limits the possibility of the gesture conforming to the sound.

EXERCISE: Hands

If excess tension persists in the forearm muscles, locking the wrist in place, practice conducting with hands hanging from the wrists doggie style. Feel that you are conducting with the bottom of the wrist. If excess tension persists in the fingers, practice conducting while wiggling them.

Legs

Full power comes from full freedom. A beat gesture that conforms to a powerful sound involves complete, explosive tension of the active muscles of the arms. One of the casualties of unnecessary tension in the upper body is a fully powerful gesture, as muscles already tensed are unavailable to tense further. Without full power available from the arms it is common to compensate with the leg muscles, either bouncing on the balls of the feet, tensing and releasing the calf muscles, or bouncing by bending the knees, releasing and tensing the quadriceps muscles of the thigh.

Both kinds of rhythmic bouncing negatively affect the conductor's presence on the podium. Both also inject another, conflicting temporal element into the conductor's physical connection with the sounding beat. And both diminish the potential power of the gesture, which comes exclusively from the arms.

---

[14] Raising the hand and fingers to the level of the forearm (extension of the wrist and fingers, anatomically) and beyond is accomplished by a series of extensor muscles that attach at the outside (non-palm side) of the bones of the hand and fingers, and at the forearm and upper arm.

EXERCISES: Bouncing

Bouncing is unlikely to occur in the simple act of raising and lowering the arms freely; rather, it occurs in giving a succession of beat gestures. To gain the sensation of moving without the offending unnecessary muscle tensions, we can prevent the offending muscle from participating. So to overcome the habit of bouncing from the knees, practice conducting while kneeling on a chair. This forces the upper body to stabilize over the knees and prevents the quadriceps muscles from participating unnecessarily. To overcome the habit of bouncing on the balls of the feet, practice conducting while standing on a step or on the podium with the balls of the feet extended over, unsupported. With the weight of the body entirely on the heels, the calf muscles are prevented from participating.

Standing with the body aligned and the weight in balance—in other words, without unnecessary compensatory muscle tensions—has multiple significant advantages for the conductor. Unnecessary tension limits the possibilities of power and internal structure of gestures. Unnecessary tension from the conductor is transferred to the musicians, and it negatively affects their overall ability to perform. And unnecessary tension—often generated by a lack of trust in oneself or the musicians—also limits the conductor's ability to absorb all the sounds. Conversely, standing in balanced alignment results in a commanding presence that draws the musicians' attention. Not only does it communicate self-confidence and trust in the musicians, but standing in alignment actually generates both self-confidence from within and respect from without.[15]

---

[15] This was demonstrated in two fascinating recent studies. In "Power Posing: Brief Nonverbal Displays Affect Neuroendocrine Levels and Risk Tolerance," social psychologists Dana Carney, Amy J. C. Cuddy, and Andy J. Yap describe placing different subjects in "high-power" and "low-power" positions for a period of two minutes. High-power positions were characterized by expansiveness and open limbs, while low-power positions were characterized by contractive positions and closed limbs. The authors determined that the subjects who assumed high-power positions for only two minutes showed measurable increases in confidence factors over the subjects in low-power one. And a study by Amy J. C. Cuddy, Peter Glick, and Anna Beninger, "The Dynamics of Warmth and Competence Judgments, and Their Outcomes in Organizations," determined that people with high-power postures are actually perceived as "more skillful, capable, and competent."

Patterns

Sounding beats do not roll out in a homogeneous succession; they are organized largely in groupings of two and three, with an implied stress on the first beat of each group. As a result, most music is notated in bars of two beats, three beats, or four beats (two groups of two).

Conductors can also organize beat gestures into groupings by altering the angle of the descent to produce gestures with differing inherent strengths. The inherent strength of a conductor's beat is a function of the strength of its *impulse*, the muscle tension that stops the descent and marks the beginning of the gesture. The strength of the impulse depends on the strength of the descent that precedes it. The strongest descent is straight down, perpendicular to the ground, in accordance with gravity; as a result, the impulse that follows a perpendicular descent is the strongest. A diagonal descent incorporating an external rotation of the upper arm—away from the center of the body—is inherently weaker than a perpendicular descent, so the impulse that follows an outward descent is weaker. And a diagonal descent incorporating an internal rotation—in toward the center of the body—is weaker still, so the impulse that follows an inward descent is the weakest. On the basis of these three differing inherent strengths of descending motions, it is possible to organize beat gestures within patterns that conform approximately to the implied stress structures of bars.[16]

Patterns are frequently described and illustrated as looping motions, with beat gestures of varying sizes and beginning at varying heights. In fact, though, learning to form patterns with gestures of a uniform size that begin on the same horizontal plane is critical to our effectiveness.

---

[16] The stress within a bar is implied, not necessarily actual; correspondingly, the strength of a beat gesture within a pattern is inherent, not necessarily actual. The actual strength of the beat gestures corresponds to the actual structure of volume of the sounded bar, which is as likely to go against the implied stresses as to follow them. For example, emphasis could well come on the second beat of a group of two. A sounded structure of volume that goes against the implied metrical stresses creates additional energy.

> ### ESSENTIAL PRINCIPLE: V not U
>
> As the arm travels through the pattern, the top and bottom of every beat forms an angle, not a loop. Looping motions preclude the possibility of a gesture having an identifiable internal structure that enables it to conform to the character of the musical beat.[17]

Alla Breve Pattern

A bar of two beats, strong–weak (S–w), is conducted in an *alla breve pattern*. Figure 3.1 illustrates an alla breve pattern in the right arm.[18] The alla breve pattern consists of a perpendicular descent to an inherently strong first impulse (beat 1) and a diagonally inward descent to an inherently weaker second impulse (beat 2). After the perpendicular descent to beat 1 of the pattern, the ascent travels diagonally outward to allow the inward descent of the weaker beat 2; the ascent of beat 2 is perpendicular to allow the perpendicular descent to the succeeding beat 1. In an alla breve pattern, beats 1 and 2 begin at the same point.

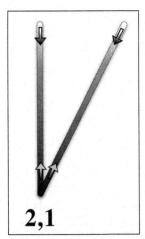

Figure 3.1. Alla breve pattern in the right arm.

---

[17] A loop at the bottom of the gesture obscures the temporal point at which it begins; a loop at the top of the gesture obscures the temporal point at which the descent begins. Perhaps counterintuitively, this is equally true of legato beat gestures.

[18] The pattern diagrams were produced by Philip Emory.

EXERCISE: Alla Breve Pattern

Start with the hands at the height of an ascent, and check for freedom of the arms, by yourself or with a partner. Descend slowly straight down to the basic position; this is the point at which beat 1 begins.

The ascent of beat 1 incorporates an external rotation of the shoulder, describing a diagonal line out from the center of the body. Go slowly, freeze at the top, and check for freedom of your arms. Be particularly careful that you have not lifted your elbows by tensing the medial deltoids on the way up; if the medial deltoids are free, the elbows will be in a line from the wrist to the shoulder, with the elbows inside the hands (i.e., closer to the body).

The descent retraces the diagonal line in reverse, returning to the basic position, which at this point is the beginning of beat 2. At the height of the previous ascent the elbows will have moved outward to a degree; be sure they do not stay there but rather remain at their lowest point through the diagonal descent. You may want to think of the elbows leading the descent. The ascent of beat 2 returns to the starting point.

Continue tracing each of the four legs of the pattern, freezing at the end of each ascent and descent to check for freedom of the arms. Go slowly, and avoid the temptation of putting beats in a musical context, which will come in chapter 4. See video demonstration 3.10.

Triangle Pattern

A bar of three beats, strong–weak–weak (S–w–w), is conducted in a *triangle pattern*. Figure 3.2 illustrates a triangle pattern in the right arm. The triangle pattern consists of a perpendicular descent to an inherently strong first impulse (beat 1), a diagonally outward descent to an inherently weaker second impulse (beat 2), and a diagonally inward descent to an inherently weaker third impulse (beat 3).[19] After the perpendicular descent to beat

---

[19] Within a three-beat bar there is no difference in implied stress between beats 2 and 3. However, within the triangle pattern, beats 2 and 3 are inherently successively weaker. The only other possibility would be to give two successive inward descents, which is potentially confusing as beats 2 and 3 would not be well differentiated.

1 of the pattern, the ascent travels straight upward to allow the diagonal outward descent to the weaker beat 2; the ascent of beat 2 is diagonally outward to allow the diagonal inward descent to beat 3; and the ascent of beat 3 is slightly inward to allow the perpendicular descent to the succeeding beat 1. On the horizontal plane, beat 1 begins at the bottom of the perpendicular descent, beat 2 begins to the outside, and beat 3 begins close to beat 1.

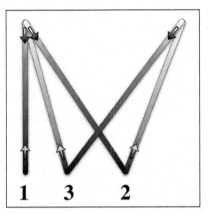

Figure 3.2. Triangle pattern in the right arm.

EXERCISE: Triangle Pattern

Start with the hands at the height of an ascent, and check for freedom of the arms, by yourself or with a partner. Descend slowly straight down to the basic position; this is the point at which beat 1 begins.

The ascent of beat 1 in a triangle pattern is straight up. The descent to beat 2 incorporates an external rotation of the shoulder and thus describes a diagonal line. Beat 2 begins at a point on a horizontal plane outside the center of the body from beat 1. Again be particularly careful through the descent that the medial deltoids are not tensed; if the medial deltoids are free during the descent to beat 2, the elbows will continuously be in a line between the wrist and shoulder, and at the end of the descent the elbows will be "inside" the hands (closer to the body).

> The ascent of beat 2 continues in an outward direction, describing a diagonal (similar to the ascent of beat 1 in an alla breve pattern). Beat 3 begins at a point on a horizontal plane close to beat 1. The diagonal descent to beat 3 incorporates an internal rotation of the upper arm. The ascent of beat 3 incorporates a slight inward rotation to return to the starting point above beat 1.
>
> Continue tracing each of the six legs of the pattern, freezing at the end of each ascent and descent to check for freedom of the arms. See video demonstration 3.11.

Cross Pattern

A bar of four beats, strong–weak–somewhat strong–weak (**S–w–S–w**), is conducted in a *cross pattern*. Figure 3.3 illustrates a cross pattern in the right arm. The cross pattern consists of a perpendicular descent to an inherently strong first impulse (beat 1), a diagonally inward descent to an inherently weaker second impulse (beat 2), a diagonally outward descent to a somewhat stronger third impulse (beat 3), and a diagonally inward descent to an inherently weaker fourth impulse (beat 4). After the perpendicular descent to beat 1 of the pattern, the ascent travels upward to allow the inward descent to the weaker beat 2; the ascent of beat 2 is upward to allow the outward descent to the somewhat strong beat 3; the ascent of beat 3 is outward to allow the inward descent to the weaker beat 4; and the ascent of beat 4 is slightly inward to allow the perpendicular descent to the succeeding beat 1.

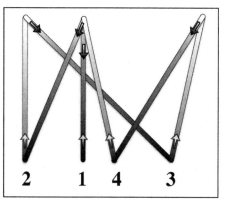

Figure 3.3. Cross pattern in the right arm.

EXERCISE: Cross Pattern

Start with the hands at the height of an ascent, and check for freedom of the arms. Descend straight down to the basic position; this is the beginning of beat 1.

The ascent of beat 1 in a cross pattern is straight up. Beat 2 begins at a point on the horizontal plane inside beat 1, closer to the center of the body. The descent to beat 2 describes a diagonal line incorporating an internal rotation of the upper arm. Be particularly careful that you do not leave the elbows in place and rotate the forearms down; rather, allow the elbows to lead the diagonal descent.

The ascent of beat 2 is straight up. As the hands rise, if the elbows are free they fall on the way up. It is important to check for freedom at the height of the ascent of beat 2 to be sure the elbows have remained in their lowest position. Beat 3 begins at a point on the horizontal plane outside beat 1. The descent to beat 3 describes an outward diagonal line. Be careful that the hands cross over the elbows during the descent. The ascent of beat 3 continues diagonally outward; the descent to beat 4, close to beat 1 on the horizontal plane, describes an inward diagonal. The ascent of beat 4 returns to the starting point, above beat 1.

Continue tracing each of the eight legs of the pattern, freezing at the end of each ascent and descent to check for freedom of the arms. See video demonstration 3.12.

Baton

The baton giveth and it taketh away. Using a baton can be an asset, but only if the negative consequences do not outweigh the benefits. On the positive side a baton can amplify and focus the gesture, enhancing to a degree the connection between conductor and musician. As a continuation on the horizontal plane of the forearm, it increases the size of the motion. This, and perhaps the contrast of light baton against dark concert clothing or background, can increase the visibility of the conductors' gestures.[20]

---

[20] It may well go without saying, but hold the baton in the right hand. Because musicians are accustomed to seeing the baton in the right hand, it may look odd and possibly disconcerting in the left hand.

These, however, are relatively small advantages easily outweighed by common problems resulting from holding a baton. The first is excess tension in the fingers. A baton is light and should require minimal tension to hold, but many people have difficulty using one without clenching or squeezing the fingers around it. This unnecessary tension in a series of muscles of the hand and forearm significantly degrades the possibility of freedom in the arms and thus limits our ability to connect gestures to sounds.

Another common problem is over-extension of the wrist (i.e., raising the hand at the wrist above the level of the forearm), which has multiple negative consequences. To function as one with the arm, the hand extends out from the forearm on the same horizontal plane, with the possibility of further extending at the wrist (going up) as the arm ascends. See figure 3.4a.

Figure 3.4a.

Holding a baton on the same horizontal plane as the forearm necessarily results in some further extension of the hand at the wrist. Note the decreased angle between hand and forearm at the wrist in figure 3.4b.

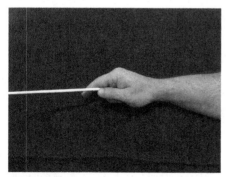

Figure 3.4b.

Extending the pronated hand at the wrist is accomplished by extensor muscles in the forearm. The more extended the wrist, the more tense these muscles are and thus the possibility of conforming gesture to sound is more limited. Over-extension of the wrist is necessitated or exacerbated by a knob or other protuberance at the end of the baton. Note the more extreme angle of wrist to forearm in figure 3.4c, as the baton extends out in the horizontal plane of the forearm.

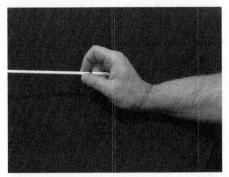

Figure 3.4c.

A baton should amplify the motion of the arm, not conflict with it. Because the baton is held in the hand it becomes an extension of the hand, so it is critical that motion of the hand at the wrist is in accord with that of the arm. If the wrist is over-extended there is little or no possibility of extending further, so the hand cannot join the arm in extending as the arm ascends. If the wrist is flexible at all it can only move down, as illustrated in figure 3.4d. This invariably results in a conflict between hand and arm, as the baton continues downward while the arm is ascending.

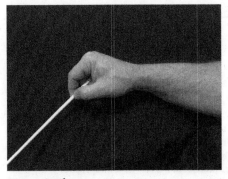

Figure 3.4d.

It also results in significant conflict between the speed of the tip of the baton and that of the arm. As the wrist flips the hand moves both considerably faster and at a more variable speed than does the arm.

PRACTICAL MATTER: Holding the Baton

Holding a baton with minimal tension as an extension of the arm is relatively simple. See video demonstration 3.13.

1. Find (or make) a baton without a handle.[21]
2. Supinate the hand (turn it palm up).
3. Place the end of the baton in the center of the palm.
4. Lay the baton diagonally across the first two fingers.
5. Flex the thumb over to hold the baton against the two fingers.
6. Pronate the hand (turn it palm down).
7. Adjust the baton so it is comfortable, with the least possible extension of the wrist upward from the forearm.

In this way, the only tension in holding the baton is minimal contraction of the thumb muscles.[22] The benefit of using a baton outweighs this small cost in extra tension.

Caution: forcing the baton out in a straight line from the forearm has a significant cost and little advantage. Held as described above, the baton naturally angles off slightly to the left. This is fine. Forcing the wrist to the side so the baton extends straight out from the forearm is accomplished by two long muscles attached to the palm and the upper arm.[23] Tension in these muscles limits the ability of the arm to connect freely with the sounds.

---

[21] To make a handle-less baton, begin with a white, cork-handled baton and remove most of the cork. For security of grip leave the black plastic O-ring and a few bits of the cork attached to the stick. Compared to the truly beautiful professionally made artisan batons with polished-wood knobby protuberances, such a stick is not only far more functional, it is also far less expensive!

[22] Specifically the adductor pollicis and flexor pollicis brevis.

[23] These muscles are the extensor carpi ulnaris and flexor carpi ulnaris.

PRACTICAL MATTER: Excess Tension

Holding a baton with your right arm in basic position, wrap your left hand around the forearm near the elbow. Squeeze your thumb and first two digits tightly together, and note the increased tension in the muscles of the forearm. In the same position, squeeze the third and fourth digits tightly into your palm, and note the additional tension in the forearm muscles. Now extend the wrist joint upward as far as possible, and note the additional tension in the muscles of the forearm. Be conscious of holding the baton without this unnecessary tension that prevents the arm from conforming gestures to sounds.

EXERCISE: Dropping the Baton

A good way to release an overly tight grip is by dropping the baton. Using only the palm muscles of the thumb to hold the baton against the first two fingers as described above, give a sharp, descending beat. Allow the baton to slip from the fingers and fall to the ground. Now give a similarly sharp, descending beat, with just enough tension of the thumb against the fingers so the baton does not fall.

Finally, if you are unable to hold a baton without unnecessary extra tension, I recommend going baton-less, at least until the sensation of raising and lowering the arms freely is ingrained. After that, learning to hold a baton without excess tension is more easily accomplished. And there is no shame in conducting without a baton; in fact, musicians rarely notice.[24]

---

24 To demonstrate this to skeptical students in a master class, I asked the orchestral musicians how many of the ten conductors had used a baton and how many had not, and the guesses were both wildly varied and largely inaccurate. As a rule, musicians don't know and don't care if the conductor uses a baton.

Summary

Our function as conductor, the most influential musician onstage, is to empower the musicians to their most moving, most beautiful performance. We do this by providing visual confirmation of the sounds to the musicians, whose primary responsibility is to the demands of the sounds. The conductor, also responding to the demands of the sounds, uses the unencumbered body to effect a full physical manifestation of the musicians' physical response to those sounds. In other words, we respond to the sounds physically just as musicians do in the act of playing. We have the disadvantage of participating in the music making only by moving our bodies and the advantage of having the physical and mental freedom to respond completely.

To be maximally effective we stand with the body in alignment and in balance, which enables us to eliminate unnecessary tensions, command attention, and project confidence, competence, and trust. Unnecessary tensions—in the muscles of the upper body, of the legs, the hands, the neck, and the head—limit our ability to conform our gestures to the sounds and thus to influence them. On the basis of the relative inherent strength of descending motions—straight down, down and diagonally outward, and down and diagonally inward—we can form our gestures within one of three fundamental patterns, conforming to the metrical organization of the sounds. It is essential that we learn to move freely through each leg of the patterns, unencumbered by unnecessary tension, and in particular to hold the baton with minimal tension.

CHAPTER FOUR

BE THE MUSIC

Applying the Free Body in the Service of a Maximally Beautiful Performance

Our consideration of conducting technique brings us full circle back to beauty. The highest experience of musical beauty requires a sound object that can be perceived as singular. The controlling element of singularity is the dynamic structure: specifically, the creations and releases of energy that result in a hierarchy of groupings, within which—to the extent possible—the energy and the music end at the same time. The performer creates the dynamic structure using principally inflections of volume and rhythmic density (the temporal distance between tones). The conductor influences the dynamic structure by conforming physical gestures principally to these same two components of the sounds: temporality and volume.

Instrumentalists use their bodies to hold an instrument and to produce the sounds, by bowing, blowing, fingering, stroking, and so on; singers maneuver their bodies for optimal operation of lungs and vocal cords. Beyond the immediate physical demands of producing sounds, musicians in the act of making music move in association with those sounds: all do it internally, and most do it to some degree externally. For chamber musicians it is this physical manifestation of the sounds that provides a visual confirmation of their audial connection. Imagine, though, a musician without an instrument to play, who could give over his or her body fully to the sounds; that musician is the conductor. Freed from the physical demands of creating the sounds, the conductor's motions constitute a full upper-body actualization of the players' necessarily limited physical manifestations of the sounds.

Of course, the conductor's physical actualization of the sounds is also limited. For example, we cannot produce gestures that connect to inflections of pitch or to balance. But we can effectively influence the sounds if—to the extent possible—we can *be the music*, conforming our physical motions to the temporality and volume of the sounds, as well as to some extent the sound quality.[1] This, in a nutshell, is conducting technique.

Temporality

The three most basic elements of temporal organization of music are pulse, beat, and meter. A pulse—singular—is the smallest recurring incidence of energy; the pulse—collective—is the periodicity of pulses. A beat is the sound that takes place from the beginning of one pulse to the beginning of the next.[2] Meter is the organization of beats into small, usually regular groupings. The previous chapter introduced the patterns within which we conform our gestures to the meter. Going further, perhaps the most critical component of effective conducting technique is conforming the gestures to the internal structure of the beats.

Every beat begins with a pulse; every pulse has duration. Every beat has a character, given by the relationship of pulse to beat. A beat in which the pulse takes up the first half has a duple legato character, or a 1:2 proportion of pulse to beat. Example 4.1 illustrates quarter-note beats with a duple legato character. Each pulse (crossed noteheads) has the duration of one full eighth note, or one half of a beat.

---

[1]   In very limited circumstances we can also reflect register in our body.
[2]   The word *beat* has two different but related meanings. In the context of the sound, I use the term *musical beat* or *sounding beat* or sometimes simply *beat*. In the context of the physical motion associated with the musical beat, I use the term *beat gesture* or sometimes simply *beat*.

Example 4.1.

A beat in which the pulse takes up the first third has a triple legato character, or a 1:3 proportion of pulse to beat. Example 4.2 illustrates quarter-note beats with a triple legato character. Each pulse has the duration of one full triplet eighth note, or one third of a beat.

Example 4.2.

A beat in which the pulse takes up the first quarter has a duple staccato character, or a 1:4 proportion of pulse to beat. Example 4.3 illustrates quarter-note beats with a duple staccato character. Each pulse takes one sixteenth note, or one quarter of a beat.

Example 4.3.

A beat in which the pulse takes up the first sixth has a triple staccato character, or a 1:6 proportion of pulse to beat. Example 4.4 illustrates quarter-note beats with a triple staccato character. Each pulse takes one sextuplet, or one sixth of a beat.

Example 4.4.

Musicians respond physically to the temporality of the sounds on multiple levels. They respond not only to the succession of beats; they also respond to the character of the beats: to the internal structure. Such physical motions, if visible, may be subtle. But string players connecting to a passage in a duple legato character may well move the instruments halfway through the beat. Wind players connecting to a triple legato passage may make a discernible movement of the instrument—or perhaps just the elbows—in the final third of the beat. So too the visible movements by singers—for example, of the shoulder or the arms—will reflect the internal structure of the beat.

EXERCISE: Musicians' Physical Response to Sounds between the Beats

Observe fine performers with excellent rhythm in the act of rehearsing or performing—either in person or with Internet videos—and pay close attention to their physical responses to sounds. All musicians respond physically beyond the motions necessary to produce sound, but some will do so more visibly than others. Identify those whose external motions are visible, and pay particular attention to the motions that happen *between* the beats as they connect to the character of the beat.

The Beat Gesture

On the most fundamental level of the conductor's actualization of the temporality of the sounds is the beat gesture: a discrete motion of the arm corresponding to the musical beat. Virtually every beat gesture given by virtually every conductor consists of a single ascending and descending motion of the arm. Therefore, virtually every beat gesture given by virtually every conductor has an internal temporal structure. A beat gesture begins with muscle tension or *impulse* that accomplishes the change in direction from descending to ascending motion; the impulse has a duration that stands in a relationship to the duration of the full beat gesture. The *descent* begins when the ascent stops and continues until the next impulse begins; the duration of the descent also stands in a relationship with the duration of the entire beat gesture.

Just as musicians connect to the sounds with physical motions that reflect both the succession of beats as well as their internal character, conductors can achieve a secure, locked-in connection between beat gesture and musical beat at the most fundamental level by synchronizing the temporal structure of the beat gesture with the character of the musical beat. Conversely, since every beat gesture has an internal structure and every musical beat has an internal structure, if the internal structure of the beat gesture conflicts with that of the musical beat, a significant degree of connection between the two is lost. And lost along with the connection is a significant degree of the capacity of that gesture to influence the sound.

We can synchronize the temporal structure of the beat gesture with that of the musical beat by conforming both the impulse and the descent of the beat gesture to the character of the musical beat.

ESSENTIAL PRINCIPLE: All Beats Are Down

Because the impulse is given by the muscle tension required to stop the descent, all beats are down; in other words, all beats are initiated from a downward motion. Even legato gestures begin with a slight sinking into the beginning of the beat; in a triple legato gesture, in fact, the sinking is the impulse.

Note that conductors whose arms are not free from unnecessary tension are compelled to give staccato beat gestures as up-spasms—gestures initiated with an upward motion. The muscles that stop the descent are the same ones that raise the arms. With these muscles already tensed during the descent, any additional sharp muscle tensing tends to generate an upward motion of the arm. An up-spasm with constant arm tension cannot conform fully to a staccato musical beat, because the internal structure of the gesture results from the temporal relationship of the tension to the freedom: limited freedom, limited structure. Moreover, gestures that are up-spasms prevent even the most basic direct association between gesture and sound, as the two do not start together: the beginning of the sounding beat actually begins midway through the ascent.

ESSENTIAL PRINCIPLE:
The Descent Is of Primary Importance

It may be counterintuitive, but to confirm the musicians' shared sense of the pulse, connecting with them inside the beats is even more critical than connecting at the beginnings of the beats. In other words, to provide confirmation of the temporal placement of a sound on the beat, the critical component of the beat gesture is the beginning of the descent prior to that sound.

ESSENTIAL PRINCIPLE:
The Arm Does Not Stop at the Top of the Ascent

Stopping the arm both requires and is necessitated by excess tension. This limits the power of the gesture, and for several reasons it precludes an internal structure of the gesture that corresponds to the sounds.[3] Note that rather than stopping, the arm feels weightless at the top of the ascent. This is particularly true of sharper-proportion (staccato character) beat gestures: the arm, free of all unnecessary tension, feels weightless at the moment when the ascent ends and descent begins, when the muscles that raise the arm are released to initiate the descent.

Duple Staccato Beats—1:4 Proportion

A musical beat with a duple staccato character has a 1:4 proportion of pulse to beat; thus the corresponding duple staccato beat gesture begins with an impulse equivalent to the first quarter of the beat and similarly ends with a descent equivalent to the final quarter of the beat. The ascent encompasses the middle two quarters. Figure 4.1 illustrates the internal structure of impulse, ascent, and descent in two successive beat gestures in a duple staccato proportion.[4]

---

[3] One reason is that functionally the descent begins when the ascent stops, thus the descent cannot correspond to the structure of the musical beat; a second reason is that the stop has a duration that does not correspond to the character of the musical beat (even if the sound stops with the beat, the dynamic structure continues), and a third reason is that tension at the height of the ascent that stops the beat inevitably results in beat gestures that are up-spasms.
[4] The beat diagrams in figures 4.1–4.4 were produced by Oliver I. Thakar.

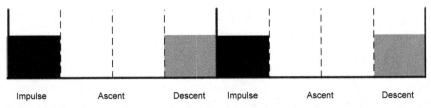

| Impulse | Ascent | Descent | Impulse | Ascent | Descent |

Figure 4.1.

EXERCISES: 1:4 Proportion

1. Give a succession of single beats (i.e., straight up and down, not in a pattern) in a 1:4 proportion. Start slowly from a basic position free of all unnecessary tension, counting out loud from "one" to "four" within each beat gesture. The impulse at the bottom of the gesture begins with the beginning of your "one," the ascent begins with the beginning of your "two," and the descent begins with the "f" sound of your "four." A common tendency is to begin the descent too soon, so be vigilant about not beginning the descent before pronouncing the "f" of "four." And it may help to think of "sinking" into the impulse. Gradually speed up the gesture, continuing to count out loud and continuing to have the impulse encompass the first quarter of the gesture, the ascent encompass the second and third quarters, and the descent the final quarter. Do not stop at the bottom—where the impulse is actually a tensing of the arm muscles to stop the descent—or at the top. Freeze periodically at the top of the ascent, making sure the arms are free of unnecessary tension. Continuing to count the internal division of the beat, return slowly to the original speed. See video demonstration 4.1.

2. A partner can help ensure that your arms are free at the top of the beat. Stand facing a partner and close your eyes as you give a succession of 1:4 proportion beats. Your partner will hold one hand in front of you at the height of the beat gesture. After a random number of beats, your partner will gently knock one of your wrists, pushing your arm out to the side. When your arm is knocked to the side, let it fly freely and stop conducting. Your arm is free of unnecessary tension if it flies to the side without resistance; however, if there is resistance to the sideways motion, you have unnecessary tension at the top of the ascent. Continue the exercise until your arms are completely free of resistance when pushed at the top of the ascent. See video demonstration 4.2.

Triple Staccato Beats—1:6 Proportion

A musical beat with a triple staccato character has a 1:6 proportion of pulse to beat; thus the corresponding triple staccato beat gesture begins with an impulse equivalent to the first sixth of the beat and similarly ends with a descent equivalent to the final sixth of the beat. The ascent encompasses the middle four sixths. Figure 4.2 illustrates the internal structure of impulse, ascent, and descent in two successive beat gestures in a triple staccato proportion.

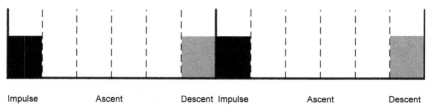

Impulse   Ascent   Descent Impulse   Ascent   Descent

Figure 4.2.

EXERCISES: 1:6 Proportion

1. As described above, give a succession of single beats in a 1:6 proportion. Start slowly from a basic position free of all unnecessary tension, counting out loud from "one" to "six" within each beat gesture. The impulse at the bottom of the gesture begins with the beginning of your "one," the ascent begins with the beginning of your "two," and the descent begins with the "s" sound of your "six." Again, be vigilant about not beginning the descent before pronouncing the "s" of "six." Gradually speed up the gesture, continuing to count out loud and continuing to have the impulse encompass the first sixth of the gesture, the ascent encompass the second through fifth, and the descent the final sixth. Freeze periodically at the top of the ascent, making sure the arms are free of unnecessary tension. Continuing to count the internal division of the beat, return slowly to the original speed. See video demonstration 4.3.

2. Have a partner perform the arm-knocking exercise described above as you give a succession of 1:6 proportion beats. See video demonstration 4.4.

Triple Legato—1:3 Proportion

In the staccato beat gestures described above, the speed of the arm is slower at the top and faster at the bottom, and the muscle tension is significant at the impulse (which specifically is an impulse of tension) and insignificant at the height of the ascent. By contrast, in legato beat gestures the ascent and descent have a relatively constant speed, and the tension in the arm muscles throughout the ascent and descent is similar, as the same muscles that raise the arm are required to resist the force of gravity on the descent. In other words, a legato gesture is legato on the basis of the rough equivalence of speed and muscle tension through the ascent and the descent.

A musical beat with a triple legato character has a 1:3 proportion of pulse to beat; thus the corresponding triple legato beat gesture begins with an impulse equivalent to the first third of the beat and similarly ends with a descent equivalent to the final third of the beat. The ascent encompasses the middle third. Figure 4.3 illustrates the internal structure of impulse, ascent, and descent in two successive beat gestures in a triple legato proportion. Note that you will sink in to the impulse, as into a pillow, rather than stop the motion of the arms.

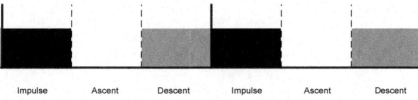

| Impulse | Ascent | Descent | Impulse | Ascent | Descent |

Figure 4.3.

EXERCISE: 1:3 Proportion

As described above, give a succession of single beats in a 1:3 proportion. Start slowly from a basic position free of all unnecessary tension, counting out loud from "one" to "three" within each beat gesture. The impulse at the bottom of the gesture begins with the beginning of your "one," the ascent begins with the beginning of your "two," and the descent begins with the "thr" sound of your "three." Gradually speed up the gesture, continuing to count out loud and continuing to have the impulse encompass the first third of the gesture, the ascent encompass the second, and the descent the final third. Freeze periodically at the top of the ascent, making sure the arms are free of unnecessary tension. Continuing to count the internal division of the beat, return slowly to the original speed. See video demonstration 4.5.

Duple Legato—1:2 Proportion

A musical beat with a duple legato character has a 1:2 proportion of pulse to beat. The corresponding duple legato beat gesture is somewhat different from the other three fundamental gestures, in that the impulse encompasses the full first half of the gesture, including the ascent. Similarly, the descent begins exactly halfway through the musical beat and encompasses the full second half. Figure 4.4 illustrates the internal structure of impulse and descent in two successive beat gestures in a duple legato proportion.

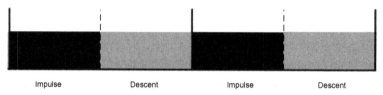

Impulse   Descent   Impulse   Descent

Figure 4.4.

EXERCISES: 1:2 Proportion

1. Repeat the exercise above with duple legato beats in a 1:2 proportion, counting out loud "one–two" within each beat gesture. The impulse begins with the beginning of your "one" and encompasses the entire ascent. The descent begins with the "t" sound of your "two." As with all beats, the impetus of the impulse is downward, not upward; as with triple legato beats, the impulse begins with a sensation of sinking in to the beat immediately before ascending.

    Gradually speed up the gesture, continuing to count out loud and continuing to have the impulse encompass the first half of the gesture, the ascent encompass the second half. Freeze periodically at the top of the ascent and make sure the arms are free of unnecessary tension. See video demonstration 4.6.

2a. With a group, begin in basic position and raise your arms slowly. Descend at the same speed, allowing your arms to travel past the basic position all the way down to your sides. The group intones "dah" when the descent has lasted precisely as long as the ascent. If your descent has the same speed as the ascent, the "dah" will come precisely when you pass to the basic position from which you began. A common tendency is for the descent to be faster than the ascent. To aid in maintaining an equivalent speed of ascent and descent, count silently from one to eight during the ascent and again during the descent. Continue the ascent through the number eight, beginning the descent on the count of one and not before.

2b. Repeat exercise 2a twice as fast, counting to four during both ascent and descent.

2c. Repeat exercise 2b twice as fast, counting to two during both ascent and descent.

2d. Repeat exercise 2c twice as fast, giving one count during the ascent and one count during the descent.

See video demonstration 4.7.

Changing Speeds

Change is most easily accomplished at the weakest point. To tear a piece of paper in a straight line we crease it, weakening the connection of the molecules. Similarly, we change the speed of the beat gesture at its weakest component: the descent. To get faster we take less time to descend from the height of the ascent to the beginning of the next impulse. To get slower we take more time to descend from the height of the ascent to the beginning of the next impulse. The impulse and the ascent that follows it take their duration from the descent that precedes them. It is critical in slowing down to resist the temptation to begin the descent too soon.

EXERCISES: Changing Speeds

The four sets of exercises below, one for each of the four basic proportions, involve conducting a group intoning and singing. The exercises aid not only in synchronizing the gestures with sounds while changing speeds, but they also help significantly to lock in each of the four basic beat gestures with its associated musical beat character. Further, they demonstrate the degree of influence a well-formed beat gesture—one with an internal structure matching that of the musical beat—can have.

Changing Speeds with Duple Staccato Musical Beats

Working with a group, conduct a succession of 1:4 proportion beats. First the group intones the syllable "dah" exactly concurrently with your impulses. It is important that they begin intoning the syllable when you begin the impulse and that they hold it through the duration of your muscle tension that stops the descent. If the group intones simultaneously with the impulses of your gestures and they are in a 1:4 proportion, the "dah" sounds will encompass the full first quarter of every beat. If, however, your impulses are too short, the "dah" syllable will likewise be too short, shorter than a full quarter of the beat.

Next the group intones the syllable "guh" concurrently with your descent. In light of the common tendency to begin the descent too soon, it is particularly critical that they begin the "g" sound exactly with the beginning of your descent. Again, if the group intones simultaneously with the descents and they are in a 1:4 proportion, the "guh" sounds will encompass the final quarter of every beat. If the descent begins too soon, the "guhs" will come early and sound more like a triple division of the beat than a quadruple division. If this happens, the ascent will need to be longer, and the descent will need to be faster.

Now divide up the group, so one half intones "dah" with the impulses and the other half intones "guh" with the descent. Assuming a quarter-note beat the combined intonations "dah . . . guh-dah . . . guh-dah . . ." should produce a rhythm of sixteenth note–two sixteenth rests–sixteenth note, as illustrated in example 4.5. See video demonstration 4.8.

Example 4.5.

dah   guh dah   guh dah   guh dah   guh

With the group singing a repeating melody in duple staccato character, such as example 4.6, conduct a series of 1:4 proportion beat gestures. As you conduct, gradually accelerate, then gradually decelerate to as slow as possible. Take care that the descent begins halfway through the second staccato eighth note of each musical beat, especially as you slow down. Remember that the new faster or slower speed begins with the descent: to slow down, take more time to get from the top of the ascent to the bottom; to speed up, take less time. And be sure the new speed of the final quarter of the beat gesture continues through the first three quarters of the next. If the gestures have an internal structure synchronous with the shared pulse of the singers, they will be able to perform the accelerando and the ensuing ritardando with precise ensemble. See video demonstration 4.9.

Example 4.6.

bom   bom   bom   bom   bom   bom   bom   bom

Changing Speeds with Triple Staccato Musical Beats

Working with a group as above, conduct a succession of triple staccato beats. First the group intones the syllable "dah" exactly concurrently with your impulse. If the impulses of your gestures are in a 1:6 proportion and the group intones simultaneously with the impulses, the "dah" sounds will encompass the full first sixth of every beat.

Then the group intones the syllable "guh" concurrently with your descent. Again it is particularly critical that they begin the "g" sound exactly with the beginning of your descent. And again if the descents of your gestures are in a 1:6 proportion and the group intones simultaneously with them, the "guh" sounds will encompass the final sixth of every beat.

Now divide up the group, so one half intones "dah" with the impulses and the other half intones "guh" with the descent. Assuming a dotted quarter-note beat, the combined intonations "dah . . . guh-dah . . . guh-dah . . ." should produce a rhythm of sixteenth note–four sixteenth rests–sixteenth note, as illustrated in example 4.7. See video demonstration 4.10.

Example 4.7.

dah   *guh dah*   *guh dah*   *guh dah*   *guh*

With the group singing a repeating melody in triple staccato character such as example 4.8, conduct a series of 1:6 proportion beat gestures. As you conduct, gradually accelerate, then gradually decelerate to as slow as possible. Take care that the descent begins halfway through the third staccato eighth note of each musical beat, especially as you slow down. Again remember that the new faster or slower speed begins with the descent: to slow down, take more time to get from the top of the ascent to the bottom; to speed up, take less time. Similarly, be sure that the new speed of the final sixth of the beat gesture obtains through the first five sixths of the next. See video demonstration 4.11.

Example 4.8.

bom *bom* *bom* *bom* *bom* *bom* *bom* *bom* *bom* *bom* *bom* *bom*

Changing Speeds with Triple Legato Musical Beats

Working with a group as above, conduct a succession of triple legato beats. The group intones the syllable "dah" concurrently with your impulse, which will encompass the full first third of every beat. Maintain the sense of sinking in with or "sitting on" the beginning of the "dah" sound. Note the common tendency to pull out of the impulse too quickly; it may help to think of the impulse as a slow stopping of the descent, with the ascent beginning on the second of the three divisions.

Continue as the group intones the syllable "guh" concurrently with your descent. If the descents of the gestures are in a 1:3 proportion and the group intones simultaneously with them, the "guh" sounds will encompass the final third of every beat.

Now divide up the group, so one half intones "dah" with the impulses and the other half intones "guh" with the descent. Assuming a dotted quarter-note beat, the combined intonations "dah . . . guh-dah . . . guh-dah . . ." should produce a rhythm of quarter note–eighth note, as illustrated in example 4.9. See video demonstration 4.12.

Example 4.9.

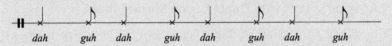

dah   guh   dah   guh   dah   guh   dah   guh

With the group singing a repeating melody in triple legato character such as example 4.10, conduct a series of 1:3 proportion beat gestures, gradually accelerating and then decelerating. Take care that the descent begins precisely with the third triplet eighth note of each musical beat, especially as you slow down. Again remember that the new faster or slower speed begins with the descent, and be sure that the new speed of the final third of the beat gesture obtains through the first two thirds of the next. See video demonstration 4.13.

Example 4.10.

la   la   la   la   la   la   la   la   la   la   la   la

Now conduct the group singing the scalar passage below using 1:3 proportion beat gestures, changing speeds as above. Take care that the descent begins on the third division of each beat, before the final sung sixteenth note, as illustrated in example 4.11. See video demonstration 4.14.

Example 4.11.

Changing Speeds with Duple Legato Musical Beats

Conduct a succession of duple legato beats. The group intones the syllable "dah" concurrently with your impulse, which will encompass the full first half of every beat. Although the impulse encompasses the ascent, maintain the downward sense of sinking in with the beginning of the "dah" sound. Continue while the group intones the syllable "guh" concurrently with your descent. If the descents of the gestures are in a 1:2 proportion and the group intones simultaneously with them, the "guh" sounds will encompass the full final half of every beat.

Now divide up the group, so one half intones "dah" with the impulses and the other half intones "guh" with the descent. Assuming a quarter-note beat, the combined intonations "dah-guh-dah-guh-dah . . ." should produce a rhythm of two legato eighth notes, as illustrated in example 4.12. See video demonstration 4.15.

Example 4.12.

dah   guh   dah   guh   dah   guh   dah   guh

With the group singing a repeating melody in duple legato character such as example 4.13, conduct a series of 1:2 proportion beat gestures, gradually accelerating and decelerating. Take care that the descent begins precisely with the second eighth note of each musical beat, especially as you slow down. See video demonstration 4.16.

Example 4.13.

la   la   la   la   la   la   la   la

Now conduct the group singing the repeating melody below using 1:2 proportion beat gestures, changing speeds as above. Take care that the descent begins on the second division of each beat, before the final sung sixteenth note, as illustrated in example 4.14. See video demonstration 4.17.

Example 4.14.

ESSENTIAL PRINCIPLE: Rhythm!

The conductor's rhythm—that is, sense of pulse—must be impeccable. A shared sense of the pulse is the musicians' first line of connection to each other, and it is the conductor's first line of connection to the musicians. Ensemble problems result from one or more musicians not sharing the same sense of the pulse; when one of those musicians is the conductor it will likely create ensemble problems!

The metronome, while not determinative of an effective tempo, is a superb tool for gaining rhythmic security. Practice conducting in private with a metronome, preferably clicking note values smaller than that of the pulse.

Twelve Fundamental Combinations

The overwhelming majority of the music we encounter as conductors is organized in bars of two, three, or four beats, in duple legato, triple legato, duple staccato, or triple staccato characters. Thus the majority of the beats we give will be in one of twelve possible combinations of proportions and patterns. Moreover, control of these twelve fundamental combinations of proportion and pattern easily transfers to other less common patterns or internal beat proportions.

ESSENTIAL PRINCIPLE: V not U

Reminder: the top and bottom of every beat forms an angle, not a loop, even for legato beats. Despite a common notion that legato beats are formed with loops, doing so limits the connection of the gesture to the sound. The legato quality of a gesture derives from the rough equivalence of the speed and muscle tension of both ascent and descent. Legato gestures formed with Vs or angles—in other words, those in which both ascent and descent begin at a discernible point—are no less legato than those formed with Us or loops at the top or bottom of the beat. Unlike looping beats, they have an internal structure that enables them to lock into the character of the musical beat, essential to maximal influence.

EXERCISES: Alla Breve Pattern

Duple Staccato Character Beats

Review the exercises for the alla breve pattern from page 48, moving slowly through each leg of the pattern. Freeze periodically to check that elbows and shoulders remain in their lowest position throughout the gesture.

Working with a group, choose one of the repeating four-note staccato figures from example 4.15, or better yet create your own. Conduct the repeating figure in an alla breve pattern, each beat having an internal 1:4 structure. Gradually change speeds, making sure that each beat retains the 1:4 proportion, that the descent begins on—not before—the fourth division of the beat, and that the changes of speed begin with the descents. See video demonstration 4.18.

Example 4.15.

Triple Staccato Character Beats

Perform the exercise described above with one of the repeating six-note staccato figures from example 4.16, or invent your own. See video demonstration 4.19.

Example 4.16.

Triple Legato Character Beats

With legato beats in particular, be vigilant against (a) the hand functioning in opposition to the arm (continuing down at the wrist while the arm has begun its ascent), (b) forming a U at the bottom of each beat instead of a V, and (c) looping at the top of the beat gestures, so the beginning of the descent is not articulated. Any of the three reduces the possibility of synching the legato gesture with the musical beat; and none adds to the legato character of the gesture, which depends on the rough equivalence between ascent and descent of muscle tension and speed.

Perform the exercise described above with one of the repeating six-note legato figures from example 4.17, or invent your own. See video demonstration 4.20.

Example 4.17.

Duple Legato Character Beats

Perform the exercise described above with one of the repeating four-note legato figures from example 4.18, or create your own. See video demonstration 4.21.

Example 4.18.

EXERCISES: Triangle Pattern

Review the exercises for the triangle pattern from pages 49–50, moving slowly through each leg of the pattern. Freeze periodically to check that elbows and shoulders remain in their lowest position throughout the gesture.

Perform one exercise for each of the four beat characters, with a repeating figure from examples 4.19–22 sung by the group. Gradually change speeds, making sure each beat retains the appropriate proportion.

Duple Staccato Character Beats

See video demonstration 4.22.

Example 4.19.

Triple Staccato Character Beats

See video demonstration 4.23.

Example 4.20.

Triple Legato Character Beats

See video demonstration 4.24.

Example 4.21.

Duple Legato Character Beats

See video demonstration 4.25.

Example 4.22.

EXERCISES: Cross Pattern

Review the exercises for the cross pattern from page 51, moving slowly through each leg of the pattern. Freeze periodically to check that elbows and shoulders remain in their lowest position throughout the gesture.

Perform one exercise for each of the four beat characters, with a repeating figure from examples 4.23–26 sung by the group. Gradually change speeds, making sure each beat retains the appropriate proportion.

Duple Staccato Character Beats

See video demonstration 4.26.

Example 4.23.

Triple Staccato Character Beats

See video demonstration 4.27.

Example 4.24.

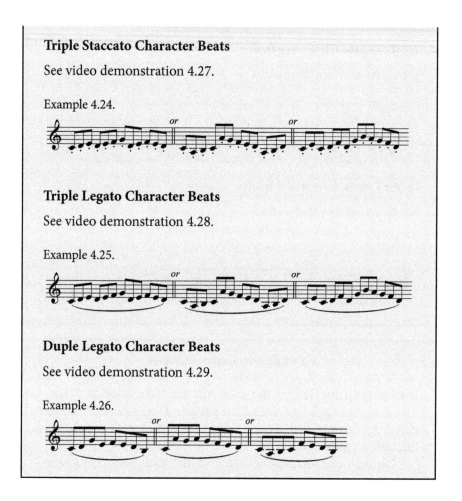

Triple Legato Character Beats

See video demonstration 4.28.

Example 4.25.

Duple Legato Character Beats

See video demonstration 4.29.

Example 4.26.

Conduct the Pulse

A common concern is what note value to assign the beat gesture: "is it in two or in four?" "in six or in two?" and so on. Simply put, *conduct the pulse.* Give one impulse (i.e., one full beat gesture) for each pulse. Note that the time signature may or may not reflect the pulse. To determine the pulse—with closed eyes and freed body and mind—hear the music internally and walk or even dance to it. The regular motions of your body synchronize with the regular injections of energy that characterize the musical passage; that is the pulse . . . conduct that.

Issues that may affect the pulse include volume and speed. The pulse of a passage played at a slower speed may have a quicker periodicity than that of the same passage played faster. For example, if the pulse of the slower performance is the quarter note, that of the faster one may be the half note. Similarly, the pulse of a passage sounding at a *forte* dynamic may have a quicker periodicity than the same material *piano*: for example, if the pulse of the loud passage is the quarter note, that of the soft passage might be the half note.

Another concern is when to change the note value of the beat gesture in a ritard or an accelerando. Again the simple rule is to *conduct the pulse*. When changing to a shorter beat value as a result of a ritard, it is essential for the first of the new beat gestures to have essentially the same duration as the equivalent division of the previous beat. For example, when the slowing tempo results in a change of the pulse from the half note to the quarter note, the first quarter note of the new pulse is virtually the same speed as the previous quarter note, so the new beat gesture is essentially twice as fast as the previous one. In an accelerando, it is helpful to conceive of reaching the new tempo a bar or so before the new faster section.

EXERCISES: Ritard with Changing Pulse

Example 4.27. Brahms, *Variations on a Theme by Haydn*.

Consider the final eleven bars of Johannes Brahms's *Variations on a Theme by Haydn*, illustrated in example 4.27.

1. Listen to different recordings, hearing all the tones, and find the pulse, again by moving or dancing to the sounds with open ears and closed eyes. Note when the pulse changes from the half note to the quarter note and—depending on the extent of the ritard—possibly to the eighth note.
2. Now perform the same exercise without a recording, hearing the tones internally.
3. Finally, stand still and conduct the passage, hearing the tones internally. Should you find that the pulse changes from the half note to the quarter note in the middle of bar 464, repeat the inward descent of the alla breve pattern. Should you find the pulse changes from a quarter note to an eighth note in bar 466, repeat the descents of the cross pattern as appropriate. Take note of the character of each musical beat and the corresponding proportion of the beat gestures.

EXERCISES: Accelerando with Changing Pulse

Example 4.28. Beethoven, Symphony no. 5, mvt. 4.

Consider the accelerando from Ludwig van Beethoven's Symphony no. 5, movement 4, measures 350–65, illustrated in example 4.28. Perform the same exercises as above:
1. Listen to different recordings, hearing all the tones, and find the pulse. Note when the pulse changes from the half note to the whole note.
2. Now perform the same exercise without a recording, hearing the tones internally.

3. Finally, stand still and conduct the passage, hearing the tones internally. Take note of the character of each musical beat and the corresponding proportion of the beat gestures.

Compound Patterns

Bars with more than four beats are conducted in either a triangle or a cross pattern with one or more descents repeated, as determined by the structure of the bar. The most common such bar is of six beats in two groups of three, with implied stresses on beats 1 and 4 (S–w–w–S–w–w). It is given in a cross pattern with two descents repeated, as illustrated in figure 4.5. As in all patterns, the strong beat 1 is approached by a perpendicular descent, and the somewhat strong beat 4 is approached by the outward descent of the cross pattern. The weaker beats 2 and 3 are approached by a repeated inward descent. To enable the repeated descent to beat 3, the outward ascent of beat 2 retraces the path of the previous descent. Beat 5, weaker than beat 4, is approached by a repeated outward descent, the repeated gesture rendering the succeeding impulse somewhat weaker. To enable the repeated descent to beat 5, the inward ascent of beat 4 retraces the path of the previous descent. Beat 6 is approached by inward descent, enabled by the outward ascent of beat 5.[5] See video demonstration 4.30.

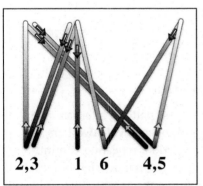

Figure 4.5. A six-beat pattern in the right arm.

---

[5] Conducting a bar of six beats divided in two groups of three beats with a "Christmas tree" pattern—alternating inward and outward descents—stands in conflict with the implied structure of the bar. The alternating inward and outward descents create inherently strong outward gestures on beats 1, 3, and 5, resulting in an inherent stress structure of three groups of two beats, in conflict with the two-groups-of-three structure of the bar.

A bar of five beats divides into a group of two beats and a group of three. It is given in a cross pattern with one descent repeated. If the bar divides into a group of two followed by a group of three (S–w–S–w–w), the somewhat strong beat 3 is approached by outward descent, which is then repeated. If the bar divides into a group of three followed by a group of two (S–w–w–S–w), the inward descent to beat 2 is repeated, so the somewhat strong beat 4 can be approached by the outward descent.

The principle of approaching stronger beats with outward descents and weaker beats with inward or repeated descents holds for any bar with more than four beats. For example, a bar with nine beats divided in three groups of three beats is conducted in a triangle pattern, with the perpendicular descent to beat 1 repeated twice, the outward descent to beat 4 repeated twice, and the inward descent to beat 7 repeated twice.

Mixed Meters

Mixed-meter bars—those with beats of differing metric values—are conducted with one of the three patterns. For example, a bar in $\frac{5}{8}$ meter with a pulse of two beats is conducted with an alla breve pattern, one beat with a value of a quarter note, the other of a dotted quarter. A bar in $\frac{7}{8}$ meter likely has three beats conducted in a triangle pattern. Two beats have the value of a quarter note, one beat has the value of a dotted quarter, with the order again determined by the musical content.

EXERCISES: Mixed Meters

Alternating Beat Values in a Cross Pattern

Conducting bars of four beats with a cross pattern, alternate two bars of quarter-note beats in a 1:4 proportion with two bars of dotted quarter-note beats in a 1:6 proportion, repeating continuously, as illustrated in example 4.29. The internal division of both beats remains a constant sixteenth note. Continue with one bar of quarter-note beats alternating with one bar of dotted quarter-note beats. Continue with two quarter-note beats alternating with two dotted quarter beats. Switch so that beats 1 and 2 have the value of the dotted quarter and beats 3 and 4 have the value of the quarter note. Next alternate one quarter-note beat with one dotted quarter beat. See video demonstration 4.31.

Example 4.29.

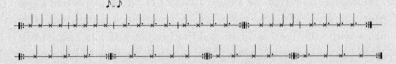

Alternating Beat Values in a Triangle Pattern

Conducting bars of three beats with a triangle pattern, alternate two bars of quarter-note beats in a 1:4 proportion with two bars of dotted quarter-note beats in a 1:6 proportion, repeating continuously, as illustrated in example 4.30. The internal division of both beats remains a constant sixteenth note. Continue with one bar of quarter-note beats alternating with one bar of dotted quarter-note beats. Continue with one quarter-note beat alternating with one dotted quarter beat. Successive bars will alternate beginning with a quarter or dotted quarter beat. See video demonstration 4.32.

Example 4.30.

Elongated Three

In a cross pattern, conduct beats 1, 2, and 4 with a quarter-note value and beat 3 with a dotted quarter value while stamping continuous quarter notes, as illustrated in example 4.31. It is important to maintain the internal structure of the beats, with quarter-note beats having a 1:4 proportion and dotted quarter beats having a 1:6 proportion. See video demonstration 4.33.

Example 4.31.

Histoire du Soldat

Igor Stravinsky's *Histoire du Soldat* offers excellent examples of mixed meters, especially in the "Soldier's March," "Airs by a

Stream," "Royal March," "Petit Concert," "Devil's Dance," and "Triumphal March of the Devil." Practice conducting each of these movements, beating the meter while stamping continuous quarter notes with your feet, as illustrated in example 4.32 (stamping indicated by crossed noteheads). Some bars will begin with beats coinciding with stamps; others will begin with beats between stamps.

NB: the $\frac{7}{16}$ bar in "Airs by a Stream" creates a small complication. Start the movement by stamping between the beats, so that feet and arms land together at the beginning of the $\frac{7}{16}$ bar. For the duration of that bar give an extended beat with both feet and arms, and land both together on the next downbeat. The $\frac{3}{16}$ bar in the "Triumphal March" creates a similar complication. Start the movement by stamping between beats to land both feet and arms together at two bars before rehearsal 9. For the second beat of that bar give a single extended beat that incorporates the $\frac{3}{16}$ bar, and land both feet and arms together on the next downbeat.

Example 4.32.

Gather seven or more colleagues to "sprechstimme" through these five mixed-meter movements. Switch parts, so each participant has an opportunity to conduct the ensemble and each has an opportunity to "sing" each of the seven parts.

Changing Speeds

Create a repeating mixed-meter figure of three or four staccato beats, or pick one of the figures below from example 4.33. Using a triangle or cross pattern as appropriate, conduct a group singing the repeating figure. Gradually change speeds, making sure each beat retains the appropriate proportion. See video demonstration 4.34.

Example 4.33.

Independence of the Arms

As a matter of convention, conductors give beat gestures with the right arm, and thus the pattern diagrams in chapter 3 illustrate the motion of the right arm. Most often the left arm will mirror the right, moving simultaneously in opposite horizontal directions.[6] However, the ability to move the left arm independently is invaluable, for example, to provide emphasis, underscore legato (with a beat-less motion), invite a player entrance, or connect with a differently shaped line from that of the right arm.

Example 4.34 is an excerpt from Beethoven's Symphony no. 8, movement 1, bars 40–42. This hemiola passage has four two-beat groupings within a meter of three beats per bar. In conducting the passage, the right hand continues in a triangle pattern, but the left hand may well emphasize the hemiola with strong descending gestures on each dotted eighth note.

Example 4.34. Beethoven, Symphony no. 8, mvt. 1.

Example 4.35 presents bars 16–22 of Mozart's Symphony no. 40, movement 1. Energy builds to the downbeat of bar 20; the descending bassoon half notes beginning in bar 20 get softer to resolve that energy. Simultaneously with the decreasing bassoon volume, violins begin a phrase at the pickup to bar 21 that increases in volume. The right hand can give beats of decreasing size or height to connect with the bassoon descent, while the left hand (closest to the violins) can rise with the rising volume of the violins.

Example 4.35. Mozart, Symphony no. 40, mvt. 1.

---

6 The common proscription of mirroring is difficult to justify.

Similarly, example 4.36—a five-bar passage from Beethoven's Symphony no. 2, movement 1—illustrates alternating phrasing inflections in different instrument groups. The direction of the volume of the violin line (decreasing in bars 12 and 14, increasing in bars 13 and 15) conflicts with that of the flute and bassoon line (decreasing in bars 13 and 15). The left hand can descend with the decreasing volume of the violins in bar 12 and rise with the increasing volume in bar 13, while the right hand is descending in bar 13 with the decreasing volume of flute and bassoon.

Example 4.36. Beethoven, Symphony no. 2, mvt. 1.

ESSENTIAL PRINCIPLE: Don't Stop the Right Arm

A common bad habit is for conductors to stop conducting with the right arm when they are making a gesture with the left arm. Independence of the arms comes when both arms serve different functions simultaneously.

EXERCISES: Independence of the Arms

1. With beats of the same duration in each arm, conduct an alla breve pattern in one arm concurrently with a triangle pattern in the other. See video demonstration 4.35.
2. Conduct polyrhythms: for example, three beats in a triangle pattern in one arm against four beats in a cross pattern in the other, with the downbeats coinciding. Also try three against two and five against three. See video demonstration 4.36.

Volume

No music worth hearing is static; energy is always either growing or receding. Performers' principal means of creating the dynamic structure on a local level is with inflections of volume. A conductor's effectiveness depends to a significant degree on his or her ability to incorporate volume—and specifically changing volume—in the gestures.

Volume can be incorporated into the conductor's physical manifestation of the sounds in two ways: size and vertical placement. Size is the distance covered from the lowest to the highest point of the beat gesture; vertical placement is the height at which the impulse begins.

Our first consideration is the overall volume level of the sounds, which is reflected in the size: the louder the volume, the bigger the gesture; the smaller the volume, the smaller the gesture. The second consideration is vertical placement, an invaluable tool with inflections of volume. Without altering the size of the gesture, we can reflect growing inflections of volume with increasingly higher beats and decreasing inflections with successively lower ones. Changing vertical placement is generally applicable in softer passages, as loud passages take larger gestures with little room to alter the height at which they begin.

Essential Principle: Uniformity of the Size of the Beat

Absent a musical context, all beats are of the same size, so that changing the size has significance. Common tendencies are to make the final beat of the pattern larger than the others or, with mixed-meter passages, to make the triple beat larger than the duple. These reduce effectiveness, not because musicians respond to the size and play larger beats louder but because they necessarily ignore the size of the beat. This eliminates a critical element of the connection between beat and sound and reduces the conductor's ability to influence the sound.

Essential Principle: Uniformity of the Plane of the Beat

Absent a musical context, all beats are on the same horizontal plane, so that changing the height of the plane has significance. Giving impulses at inconsistent heights (unfortunately not uncommon) also eliminates an element of the connection between beat and sound; it reduces the conductor's ability to use the height of the beat to connect with volume inflections.

Exercise: Size

As described in the exercise on changing speeds above, conduct the group singing a repeating mixed-meter figure of three or four staccato beats in a triangle or cross pattern. In addition to changing speeds, change the volume by increasing or decreasing the size of the beat. See video demonstration 4.37.

EXERCISES: Vertical Placement

1. With a group singing example 4.37, conduct it with 1:2 proportion beats in a cross pattern. Be sure the descent begins
   on the second division of each beat, before the final sung sixteenth note, as indicated by the arrows. With beats of the same
   size, gradually increase the volume by increasing the height of
   the gestures over the first two bars, and lower it over the final
   two bars as you also get slower. See video demonstration 4.38.

Example 4.37.

2. With a group singing example 4.38, conduct it with 1:3 proportion beats in a cross pattern. Be sure the descent begins on
   the third division of each beat, before the final sung sixteenth
   note, as indicated by the arrows. Again using beats of the same
   size, gradually increase the volume by increasing the height of
   the gestures over the first two bars, and lower it over the final
   two bars as you also get slower. See video demonstration 4.39.

Example 4.38.

3. Example 4.39 presents the opening four-bar phrase of Mozart's
   "Serenade no. 13," K. 525, *Eine kleine Nachtmusik*, movement 2.
   The crescendo and diminuendo signs in parentheses indicate

subtle phrasing inflections that occur within the overall *piano* dynamic. With a group performing (or singing), raise and lower your arms vertically in conjunction with the phrasing inflections. Beginning in basic position, raise your arms over the first two full bars as the passage gathers energy and grows subtly in volume; lower them over the last two full bars as the passage releases that energy. Now conduct the passage with a cross pattern, placing the beginning of each beat at the height it was in the exclusively vertical ascent and descent. Make sure the impulses begin successively higher over the first two bars and successively lower over the last two.

Example 4.39. Mozart, "Serenade no. 13," *Eine kleine Nachtmusik*, mvt. 2

Sound Quality and Register

In addition to temporality and volume, conductors can reflect the quality of the sound and, to a much lesser degree, register.

Stringed instruments and voices in particular have a significant range of quality of sound, from rich and intense to light and airy; we can connect our gestures to different sound qualities with different levels of tension in the body. For example, to connect with the rich, dark sound appropriate to late Romantic German or Russian repertoire, we can form our gestures with an added continuous degree of tension in the muscles needed to move our bodies (however, the muscles we do not need—the medial deltoids, trapezoids, and so on—remain free). And to connect with the light, transparent sound appropriate to early Classical Era music, we can form gestures with no excess tension whatsoever. Sound quality can similarly be reflected in the facial expressions: muscles tensed in connecting with richer dark sounds, free in lighter music.

Register may be reflected by the height of the gestures. Absent other higher-priority considerations, it is possible to conduct high-register sounds with gestures that are higher within the conducting space and low-register sounds with gestures that are lower. For example, absent other considerations, higher gestures have more of a direct connection with soprano tones, as lower gestures do with bass ones.

Summary

We've come to the podium with an understanding of how our musicians can bring these particular tones to life in the most magical, most moving, most beautiful way. With a free mind we open ourselves to all the sounds and only the sounds. We connect our body—aligned, balanced, and free of unnecessary tensions—to those sounds. With each musical beat we form a discrete gesture; we lock in each of those beat gestures to the sound by synchronizing its internal structure with the character of the musical beat. We form patterns of inherently stronger and weaker gestures that conform to the metrical organization of stronger and weaker musical beats. We connect the size of our gestures with the volume and the plane of the gestures with phrasing inflections. And with nuances of tensions in our body and face, we reflect the quality of sound. The range of possibilities of physical motions pales in comparison with the unlimited possibilities of sound, yet to the absolute maximal extent possible we allow our bodies to *be the music.*

In summary I return to the beginning: the goal of conducting. If the goal is to ensure a correct reading of the score, or if it is to impose a distinctive interpretation on the ensemble, then the essence of our job is using physical gestures to compel musicians to generate the sounds as we desire them. And the musicians' responsibility then is to follow our desires, which we indicate by gesturing at them.

But if we understand the possibility of that celestial, most moving experience available from sound when all the components come together into one, if we understand that musicians share that experience and are equally driven by it, if we trust the musicians and trust ourselves, then conducting is not about dictating to musicians but about empowering them . . . joining, escorting, confirming, and guiding them with physical gestures to respond to the demands of the sounds. Don't get louder because I conduct at you with increasingly bigger gestures; allow my gestures—increasingly bigger as I connect with the building energy—to connect you with and confirm our shared sense of shape. Don't slow down because I wave at you more slowly; allow my gestures—slower as I respond to the necessity of relaxing the tempo to release energy—to connect you with and confirm your own sense of that release.

The world is not perfect. Performances are rarely optimal; not all compositions allow the highest, transcendent experience; not all musicians are 100 percent open. Surprises happen in performance, someone gets lost, someone plays out of tune, someone plays too loud, the focus of our consciousness is directed to limited elements, the continuum of our consciousness of the sounds is broken on the highest level. So be it. There is beauty on all levels, and it is up to us to help bring it about, wherever, whenever, however, and to whatever extent we can, with a free mind, and a free body, being the music.

STARTING, STOPPING, AND FERMATAS

Achieving a Collective Sense of When to Begin and End the Sound

Starting

Beginning a work or movement together can be challenging for any ensemble, and so starting is a matter of particular importance for the conductor. It is commonly thought that musicians require a preparatory gesture to inform them when to begin and at what speed. In fact *the musicians know (within a very small range) when to begin, and they know (within a very small range) the speed.*

Before the performance begins, noise and activity fill the room. A signal—for example, raised arms from the conductor or a raised instrument from the leader of a chamber group—initiates quiet and stillness. In that moment of utter silence the focused consciousness of each musician enters the world of the upcoming sound. For each musician so focused, there is a moment at which the sound must begin . . . a moment before which it is too soon and after which it is too late. And within a very small range, musicians share a sense of that moment. Further, assuming that the work has been rehearsed at an effective tempo, musicians know that tempo within a very small range. Thus the conductor's preparatory gesture does not dictate the beginning point or speed of the performance; rather the conductor—whose focused consciousness is also turned toward the upcoming sound—gives a preparatory gesture for the sound to begin at his or her intuited moment. That gesture serves to confirm and synchronize the narrowly divergent individual musicians' senses of both beginning point and speed.

An effective preparatory gesture describes (or implies) a full beat. It reflects the character of the first sounding beat in internal structure, volume, and quality of sound, and it pinpoints the temporal beginning of that initial sound. The preparatory gesture—or preparation—consists of no less than one impulse and one descent and no more than one full impulse and two descents. And it occupies the position in the pattern immediately preceding that of the first musical beat.

ESSENTIAL PRINCIPLE: Know the Tempo

A preparatory beat must share the duration of the first sounding beat. In other words, it must be in tempo. Make sure you feel the pulse as you begin the preparatory beat gesture. If the beat is too slow (a common tendency), either some or all musicians will go with the slower speed, or a degree of the connection between gesture and sound—and thus between conductor and musician—will be lost.

PRACTICAL MATTER: Musicians Knowing the Tempo

Likewise, for an ensemble to start together it is important that the individual performers all have a strong sense of the tempo to come, particularly for fast works. It can be helpful to ask the musicians to audialize the tempo as they prepare to start.

ESSENTIAL PRINCIPLE: One Preparatory Beat Only

One preparatory beat that conforms to the character of the first sounding beat is sufficient to synchronize the start. If one is effective, giving an extra one is unnecessary and potentially confusing.

> need to inhale more than a single beat prior to an entrance. Instead of inhaling, try exhaling slowly as you move your arms into position to give the preparation, and form that preparatory gesture near the end of the exhalation.

Works Beginning on the Beat

At essence, preparatory gestures consist of an impulse and a descent. With works beginning on the beat we have a "free" descent to the preparatory beat. This initial descent may well be fairly short, but it helps to secure the collective understanding of the temporal beginning point. It is free in that it has no cost or downside: it will not cause musicians to enter early. Thus when the first sound comes on the beat, the preparation begins with a descent to an impulse, followed by the descent to the beat of the first sound, all within the proportion of the first sound.

On the Beat, Duple Staccato: Descent–Impulse–Descent

Example A.1. Beethoven, Symphony no. 4, mvt. 4.

Example A.1 represents the opening of Beethoven's Symphony no. 4, movement 4, Allegro ma non troppo. The two beats per bar have a duple staccato character, as the pulse is a sixteenth note in duration within the quarter-note beat; the beat gestures have a 1:4 proportion. The first sound comes on beat 1 of a two-beat bar, so the preparatory gesture consists of a descent to beat 2 of an alla breve pattern, the impulse of beat 2, and the descent to the downbeat, the first sounded beat. The component descents and impulse of the gesture each have a duration of a sixteenth note—one quarter of the quarter-note beat—conforming to the duple staccato character of the passage. See video demonstration A.1.

On the Beat, Triple Staccato: Descent–Impulse–Descent

Example A.2. Beethoven, Symphony no. 2, mvt. 3.

Example A.2 represents the opening of Beethoven's Symphony no. 2, movement 3, Scherzo: Allegro. The one-per-bar beats have a triple staccato character, as the pulse is an eighth note within the dotted half-note beat; the beat gestures have a 1:6 proportion. The first sound comes on beat 1, so the preparatory gesture consists of a descent, an impulse, and a subsequent descent to the first sounded beat. Each of the component descents and impulse has the duration of an eighth note—one sixth of the dotted half-note beat—conforming to the triple staccato character of the passage. See video demonstration A.2.

On the Beat, Triple Legato: Descent–Impulse–Descent

Example A.3. Bach, "Jesu, Joy of Man's Desiring."

Example A.3 represents the opening of "Jesu, Joy of Man's Desiring" from Bach's cantata *Herz und Mund und Tat und Leben*, BWV 147. The three beats per bar have a triple legato character, as the pulse is a triplet eighth note within the quarter-note beat; the beat gestures have a 1:3 proportion. The first sound comes on beat 1, so the preparatory gesture consists of a descent to beat 3 of a triangle pattern, the impulse of beat 3, and the descent to the downbeat, the first sounded beat. Each of the component descents and impulse has a duration of a triplet eighth note—one third of the quarter-note beat—conforming to the triple legato character of the passage. Be careful to sink into the impulse of the preparation for a full third of the beat. See video demonstration A.3.

On the Beat, Duple Legato: Descent–Impulse–Descent

Example A.4. Haydn, Symphony no. 97, mvt. 2.

Example A.4 represents the opening of Haydn's Symphony no. 97, movement 2. The four beats per bar have a duple legato character, as the pulse is an eighth note within the quarter-note beat; the beat gestures have a 1:2 proportion. The first sound comes on beat 4, so the preparatory gesture consists of a descent to beat 3 of a cross pattern, the impulse of beat 3, and the descent to beat 4, the first sounded beat. Each of the component descents and impulse of the preparatory gesture has a duration of an eighth note—one half of the quarter-note beat—conforming to the duple legato character of the passage. See video demonstration A.4.

Works Beginning between Beats

While the essence of the preparation for works beginning on the beat is one impulse and one descent, the essence of the preparation for works beginning between beats comprises those same components in reverse order: a descent followed by an impulse.

The preparation may begin with a neutral ascent, neutral in that it does not begin with an impulse but is simply a steady upward floating of the arm (a dynamic ascent can easily provoke an early entrance). The neutral ascent should be in tempo; it joins with the subsequent descent to take the time of one full beat. In other words, if the first musical beat has a duple staccato character, the neutral ascent encompasses the time of three quarters of a beat, and the preparatory descent takes the time of one quarter of a beat. During a neutral ascent it may be helpful to leave the left arm stationary until it joins the right arm for the descent and subsequent impulse.

Before the Beat, Duple Staccato Character: Descent–Impulse

Example A.5. Schumann, Symphony no. 3, mvt. 5.

Example A.5 represents the opening of Schumann's Symphony no. 3, movement 5. The two beats per bar have a duple staccato character, as the pulse is an eighth note within the half-note beat; the beat gestures have a 1:4 proportion. The preparatory gesture consists of an inward descent to beat 2 of the alla breve pattern, followed by the impulse and subsequent ascent of beat 2. The descent and the impulse each have a duration of an eighth note—one quarter of the half-note beat—conforming to the duple staccato character of the passage. The initial descent may be preceded by a neutral ascent, which would be outward (describing the ascent of beat 1 of the alla breve pattern). See video demonstration A.5.

Before the Beat, Triple Staccato Character: Ascent–Descent–Impulse

Example A.6. Mozart, Symphony no. 29, mvt. 4.

Example A.6 represents the opening of Mozart's Symphony no. 29, movement 4. The two beats per bar have a triple staccato character, as the pulse is
a sixteenth note within the dotted quarter-note beat; the beat gestures have
a 1:6 proportion. As with the Schumann example above, the preparatory
gesture consists of an inward descent to beat 2 of the alla breve pattern, followed by the impulse and subsequent ascent of beat 2. The descent and the
impulse each have a duration of a sixteenth note—one sixth of the dotted
quarter-note beat—conforming to the triple staccato character of the passage. Again, the initial descent may be preceded by a neutral ascent, which
would be outward (describing the ascent of beat 1 of the alla breve pattern).
See video demonstration A.6.

After the Beat, Duple Staccato Character: Ascent–Descent–Impulse

Example A.7. Schumann, Symphony no. 2, mvt. 2.

For works beginning shortly after the beginning of the beat, the preparatory
gesture likewise consists of a descent and an impulse, but an initial neutral
ascent is necessary. Example A.7 represents the opening of Schumann's
Symphony no. 2, movement 2. The two beats per bar have a duple staccato
character, as the pulse is a sixteenth note within the quarter-note beat; the
beat gestures have a 1:4 proportion. The preparatory gesture consists of an
outward ascent from beat 1 in the alla breve pattern and an inward descent
to beat 2, followed by the impulse of beat 2. See video demonstration A.7.

After the Beat, Triple Staccato Character: Ascent–Descent–Impulse

Example A.8. Elgar, *Variations on an Original Theme "Enigma."*

Example A.8 represents the opening of Elgar's *Variations on an Original Theme "Enigma,"* op. 36, variation 2. The one-per-bar beats have a triple staccato character, as the pulse is a sixteenth note within the dotted quarter-note beat; the beat gestures have a 1:6 proportion. The preparatory gesture consists of an ascent, a sixteenth-note descent, and a sixteenth-note impulse. See video demonstration A.8.

After the Beat, Triple Legato Character: Ascent–Descent–Impulse

Example A.9. Tchaikovsky, *Serenade for Strings*, mvt. 2.

Example A.9 represents the opening of Tchaikovsky's *Serenade for Strings*, movement 2. The one-per-bar beats have a triple legato character, as the pulse is a quarter note within the dotted half-note beat; the beat gestures have a 1:3 proportion. The preparatory gesture consists of a neutral ascent, a quarter-note descent, and a quarter-note impulse. See video demonstration A.9.

Between Beats, Duple Legato Character: Descent–Impulse

If a work in a duple legato character begins on the second half of the beat, the preparatory gesture may be simply a descent followed by an impulse; an initial neutral ascent is possible but unnecessary.

Example A.10. Mozart, *Sinfonia Concertante*, mvt. 2.

Example A.10 represents the opening of Mozart's *Sinfonia Concertante* K. 364, movement 2. The three beats per bar have a duple legato character, as the pulse is an eighth note within the quarter-note beat; the beat gestures have a 1:2 proportion. With the first sound coming on the second half of the beat, the preparatory gesture consists of an outward descent to beat 2 of the triangle pattern and the subsequent outward ascent, which is the impulse of beat 2. The first sounded eighth note coincides with the descent of beat 2. See video demonstration A.10.

After the Beat, Triple Legato Character: Descent–Impulse

Similarly, if a work in a triple legato character begins on the final third of the beat, the preparatory gesture begins with a descent to the impulse that precedes the first sound.

Example A.11. Beethoven, Symphony no. 5, mvt. 3.

Example A.11 represents the opening of Beethoven's Symphony no. 5, movement 3. The musical beats—one per bar—have a triple legato character. The pulse is a quarter note within the dotted half-note beat; the beat gestures have a 1:3 proportion. The preparatory gesture consists of a descent, an impulse, and an ascent, each with the duration of a quarter note, conforming to the triple legato character of the passage. See video demonstration A.11.

ESSENTIAL PRINCIPLE:
Preparatory Gesture in Mixed-Meter Passages

In mixed-meter passages the preparatory gesture is always a duple, even if the first musical beat is a triple. For example, for a mixed-meter work beginning with a $\frac{5}{8}$ bar, the preparatory gesture has a value of a quarter note, even if the first sounding beat has a value of a dotted quarter note.

Stopping

Just as musicians know when to start, they know when to stop. In fact, the ending point of a held sound is at least as evident as the starting point of a work or movement: a held tone is obliged to stop when the energy is played out. The conductor's cutoff serves to synchronize the very narrowly divergent individual musicians' senses of the ending point.

The cutoff of a held tone is an impulse in the character of the previous beat preceded by a vertical descent. The sound stops on the beginning of the impulse. The size of the descent is appropriate to the volume. The cutoff for a loud held tone may require an ascent prior to the descent to enable a sufficiently large gesture. See video demonstration A.12.

The cutoff for a soft held tone will likely not require an ascent and can begin from the held position. See video demonstration A.13.

NB: cutoff gestures traditionally involve some kind of curlicue, loop, or otherwise circular motion. Such gestures may look pretty, but they only muddy the internal structure of the gesture.

PRACTICAL MATTER: Fading Final Tone

When the end of a work fades to silence, for example the final
tone of Samuel Barber's *Adagio for Strings*, simply maintain a slow
ascent of the arms until the sound disappears.

PRACTICAL MATTER: Time at the End of a Movement

After the sounding of the final tone of a movement, some energy
remains. Allow the energy to dissipate completely—especially following the final sound of a slow movement—before releasing your
arms.

Fermatas

The sections above treat both starting and stopping. A fermata is simply the
reverse: stopping, then starting again. The first consideration is how long to
hold the fermata. A guiding principle of music making is that within any
grouping, the music and the energy end at the same time, to the extent possible. The function of any slowing or stretching of the tempo is to release
excess energy. So the fermata ends when the excess energy is released.

The second consideration is whether there is a break in the sound after
the fermata, and, if so, how long a break. A break is needed to allow time
for the sound to clear, for example with a soft continuation after a loud
fermata, but a break is undesirable if it interrupts the line.

Continuing after the fermata involves the same considerations as starting the beginning of a movement, with the advantage that the continuing
music comes within the context of the already established pulse.

ESSENTIAL PRINCIPLE: Give the Impulse of Each Beat Once

Whenever possible, give the impulse of each beat once and only once. The gesture for most fermatas begins with a conducted impulse; the temporal displacement of the beat is reflected either by holding at the top of the subsequent ascent or by stretching the ascent. However, when the impulse of the fermata beat is needed for starting the continuation, it is advisable to withhold that impulse from the fermata beat and simply stop at the bottom of the gesture.

Example A.12. Beethoven, Symphony no. 1, mvt. 4.

Example A.12 presents a passage toward the end of Beethoven's Symphony no. 1, movement 4, Allegro molto e vivace. The first fermata on the F♯ diminished seventh harmony continues without a significant break because the line continues. A break is necessary after the second fermata, however, to clear the sound for the ensuing *piano* sixteenth notes.

For the first fermata, give the downbeat of bar 235 and hold it at the top of the ascent. A descent to beat 2 and the beat 2 impulse prepare the downbeat of bar 236. For the second fermata stop on the downbeat of bar 237 without giving an impulse; from that position give one bar in tempo beginning with the impulse of beat 1. The impulse of beat 1 serves as the cutoff of the fermata, and the ensuing descent and impulse form the preparation of the continuation. See video demonstration A.14.

Example A.13. Beethoven, Violin Concerto, mvt. 3.

In example A.13, from Beethoven's Violin Concerto, movement 3, measures 1–12, the fermata begins on beat 2 of an alla breve pattern; the continuation comes before the next downbeat. For clarity, stop on beat 2 without giving an impulse; then give the impulse of that second beat as a preparation for the continuation. See video demonstration A.15.

Example A.14. Beethoven, Symphony no. 7, mvt. 1.

In example A.14, from the recapitulation of Beethoven's Symphony no. 7, movement 1, the first fermata comes on beat 1 of bar 299; the continuation comes before the next beat 1. The second fermata also comes on beat 1, but the continuation from the second fermata begins on beat 2 of the same bar. With the first fermata in bar 299 give the impulse and the ascent of beat 1, and stop at the top of the ascent. The descent into beat 2 and its impulse prepare the sixteenth-note continuation. To avoid giving the impulse of beat 1 twice in bar 300, stop on the downbeat at the bottom of the descent with the sounding of the second fermata, then give the triple legato impulse (1:3 proportion) of that downbeat to prepare the oboe solo beginning on beat 2. See video demonstration A.16.

ODDS AND ENDS

A Miscellany of Matters Musical, Physical, and Practical

For veteran conductors, experience will have led to solutions and workable processes for many if not all of the issues addressed in this addendum. Less practiced conductors may find the chapter particularly useful; perhaps more practiced ones will find nuggets of interest as well.

Before the Rehearsal

Marking the Parts

The more markings there are in the parts, the more the music-making process becomes visual rather than aural. String parts, however, must be bowed. The quality of sound and inflections of volume are affected by the direction, speed, weight, location on the string (closer to or farther from the bridge), location on the bow (closer to or farther from the frog), and angle of the bow (the amount of hair that contacts the string). Conductors who are string players likely have an instinctive understanding of these considerations, and non-string players should try to achieve a similarly firm grasp of the range of sound possibilities.

Principal players generally mark bowings in advance, but because they may not share the conductor's understanding of dynamic structure, the bowings may result in less than optimal phrasing inflections or

quality of sound. For this reason some conductors make sets of meticu-
lously bowed parts. However, individual players differ and string sections
differ, thus bowings are not universally optimal and often get changed
in rehearsal to suit a particular ensemble. As bowings may get changed,
many conductors find it best to accept the principals' bowings and work
out any kinks in rehearsal.

It can be helpful to notate ornaments in all parts and to mark breaths
in chorus and wind parts, either to ensure uniform articulations or to organize staggered breathing. And a chorus can benefit from marked consonant placements.[1] As a matter of practicality, however, most or all of this
can easily be accomplished in rehearsal.

Finally, marking phrasing inflections is best avoided: a musician who
makes an inflection of volume by following a written marking is less likely
to do it musically than one who hears the musical necessity.

Marking the Score

Marking the score for use in performance adds yet another layer of distance
between the conductor and the sounds. Simply put, conductors generally
use scores when they do not know the work well enough to free themselves
from it. At best, the conductor who uses a score has an intimate but insufficient knowledge of the work, and glancing at the page provides the occa-
sional reminder. In such a case the conductor's consciousness can be open
to the sounds to a degree when not taken up with looking down or turning
pages. But the more the conductor relies on the score, the more his or her
consciousness is taken up with the relationship between the sounds and
the page, and the less open she or he can be to the full musical possibilities.
And the conductor who relies on score markings, especially colorful ones,
is limited to a consciousness of sforzando (red), of crescendo (yellow), bassoon (blue), and so on; any ability to be open to the totality of the sounds
is sorely compromised.

For the conductor who comes to the performance without a score,
marking the score in the study process may be helpful, but primarily as a
reminder for future encounters with the work. An optimal phrasing inflection worked out with difficulty might be noted; the structural harmonic
progression or the climax of the movement might be indicated. While a

---

[1]   Chicago Symphony Chorus director Duain Wolfe has singers mark consonant placement if it is
    otherwise vague, for intelligibility, for a special effect, if the consonant should start before the beat
    (i.e., rolled Rs or an early F or V, especially in German), or in the case of a particular but unspecified
    release (i.e., soft or strong).

marking can be helpful in a subsequent study, no marking can substitute for again reaching an understanding of how the tones can come together to work on us in the most beautiful, most moving way.

Stage Setup

There is no perfect way to seat an ensemble onstage; there is no stage setup that does not have disadvantages. The controlling determinant is how to enable the best musical experience for the listeners. Some conductors situate each instrument or section on the basis of its individual acoustic advantage; however, to maximize musical experience, the overriding consideration must be the musicians' ability to hear each other in accordance with their musical function.

Sound waves in air are condensations and rarefactions of the air molecules, disturbances resulting from an energy source. Sound waves take time to travel, and they dissipate over time, as the energy converts to heat through the motions of the molecules. By the time a sound wave travels from its source at one end of a sixty-foot stage to the other, there is a perceptible time lag (roughly 1/20 of a second) and volume loss. In other words, the farther from the sound source, the more difficult it is to hear. For this reason, some elements of seating are common, if not quite universal.

Musicians' immediate responsibility is to join with like instruments or voices, so all members of the same section are seated in close proximity. Orchestras place first violins with first violins, flutes with flutes, woodwinds with woodwinds, and so on. Similarly, wind ensembles place woodwinds with woodwinds, brass with brass, and percussion with percussion. Most commonly, choruses group the sections together.

In principle, instrumental ensembles place the instruments with the most prominent material and the most capable players in the front or center and progress outward. In an orchestra, the string section generally forms the body of orchestral sound; the strings are situated in the most acoustically advantageous position closest to the audience. The woodwinds, generally the next musical priority, are given the next most advantageous position. Brass and percussion—with lesser musical priorities—are successively farther away.

Within the string section, first violins—who generally have the highest-priority musical material—are universally seated on the outside stage right in the most acoustically advantageous position, with *f*-holes directed out. Seating the remainder of the sections varies. Some conductors seat the second violin section on the outside stage left, to allow for a stereophonic effect between the two violin sections. Some seat the viola section on the outside, ostensibly to maximize their volume.[2] Bass sections can be found in the back, usually stage left, sometimes stage right, and occasionally across the rear of the stage.

The more standard stage setup—strings occupying a semicircle in front of the stage, with violins stage left, cellos outside stage right, and basses behind cellos—maximizes the musicians' ability to hear each other in accordance with their musical function. The first violins generally have the priority material. The second violins can fulfill their responsibility to merge their sounds with the first violins if they are in closest possible proximity to them. Similarly, the violas can fulfill their responsibility to merge with the second violins if they are in closest proximity to them, as with cellos to violas and basses to cellos.

In keeping with the orchestral arrangement of higher instruments to the conductor's left down to lower instruments to the right, I ask for choruses to be seated similarly: left-to-right sopranos, altos, tenors, basses. Other setups have women to the left, men to the right, with the lower-register section in back; or mixed seating, in which the choir is divided into individual quartets of singers. In the former it is somewhat harder for the sections to hear each other in function of overall balance; in the latter it is difficult if not impossible to achieve a unified sound within the individual sections.

Wind ensemble personnel can vary dramatically from composition to composition and group to group. Generally the guiding principles obtain: instruments with the most prominent material and the most capable players sit in the front or in the center; the ensemble fans out from there.

Seating an ensemble on risers can significantly aid the aural connection among the players and thus the balance. Bodies, music stands, and instruments between the musician and the sound source impede the sound waves, limiting the ability of a musician in the back of the hall to hear one in front. As sound travels omnidirectionally from the source, seating players on risers allows a more direct path for the sounds to reach them. This has a double benefit for the balance. In an orchestra, for example, woodwinds on risers can be heard more easily, and brass and percussion players on higher risers can more easily hear the sounds they accompany and—perhaps

---

[2] Seating violas on the outside to enhance their audibility seems a self-defeating proposition, as it points their *f*-holes—from which the sound emanates—directly away from the audience and places cellos in an acoustically advantageous position—with *f*-holes directed out. The cello is an acoustically perfect (i.e., strong), low-register instrument with a general obligation to be softer than higher-register instruments, and the viola is an acoustically imperfect (i.e., weaker) tenor instrument. Seating the inherently acoustically disadvantaged violas on the outside exacerbates the problem.

counterintuitively—as a result blend more effectively. Similarly, a large string section benefits from graduated risers for the back stands.

Onstage

Additional Preparatory Gesture

Some ensembles are accustomed to—and prefer—two preparatory beat gestures. If one preparatory gesture is sufficient, giving two beats actually limits the musicians' ability to join the sound world: it changes their focus from joining as full participants in the coming sound to following the dictates of the stick. And in practical terms, giving two full preparatory impulses will eventually provoke a musician to enter one beat early. However, in the absence of enough rehearsal time to cement a collective cognizance of the tempo, there may be occasions in which an additional gesture is helpful. One solution is to give a quick lateral motion of the right wrist one beat prior to the full preparatory gesture; this establishes a succession of beats without provoking an early entrance. A second is to actually give a full extra beat gesture with the right arm while extending the left hand in stationary "don't play yet!" mode.

Behind the Beat

Some ensembles—orchestras particularly—are accustomed to playing behind the beat, especially to begin a work. Playing behind is the only possibility musicians have to connect with each other when the conductor does not form beat gestures with a discernible internal structure. Absent a discernible structure in the preparatory gesture that synchronizes with the character of the first sounding beat, the gesture cannot confirm a collective sense of the pulse that is to come. The only available strategy for the musicians is to wait for the beat gesture to begin and to try to enter together thereafter. Of course, without the direct connection of beat gesture to sound, the conductor has less influence and is thus less effective.

Faced with an ensemble that consistently plays behind the beat, the music director or regular conductor can change the practice by consistently forming beats with an internal structure appropriate to the sounding beat and by asking musicians to trust the gesture. A guest conductor can ask but ultimately has no choice but to work with the delay. Expect the ensemble to be more behind in slower music and closer to or on the beat in faster music. It helps to understand that the musicians are unlikely to come apart, as they need to rely on listening to connect in spite of the temporal dissonance with the conductors' gestures. The best strategy for the guest conductor is to charge ahead with confidence and hope for the best.

The most effective beat gesture coincides with the sounding beat, with one notable exception: a loud, sustained chord preceded by a short pickup, such as at the opening of Beethoven's Symphony no. 2. In such a case, give a preparatory gesture as if the work starts without the pickup, and expect the short pickup note to coincide with the subsequent impulse.[3]

Cues

A cue—a physical confirmation of the temporal placement of an entrance directed to an individual musician or section—may be particularly valuable and appreciated after a long period of rests. Simple eye contact before the entrance is generally sufficient. If a gesture is appropriate, let it be an open-handed invitation rather than finger pointing. Pointing is both potentially offensive and—absent a "train wreck" or a musician who is lost—unnecessary.

Descent Articulation

Musicians connect to the pulse before the event—not just to the beat before but to the final internal division of that beat. Similarly, we assist the musicians in connecting to the pulse with a descent that encompasses that final division. In certain instances in legato passages it is valuable to articulate the beginning of the descent with particular precision—for example, with a soft brass entrance, a bass pizzicato, or a choral chord change.

It is possible to do this—without an additional motion that conflicts with the pulse—by leaving the hand in place as the forearm begins to drop at the wrist. Note that this is not a flip of the fingers or a lifting of the hand at the wrist but a subtle gesture in which the hand stays in place and the wrist starts down before the hand. The subtle but definitive drop of the wrist clarifies the temporal location of the upcoming beat by giving distinction to the beginning of the descent . . . to the second half of a duple legato beat or to the final third of a triple legato beat. While the arm begins the descent before the hand does, it is critical that both hand and arm land together at the bottom of the gesture to begin the next impulse; otherwise

---

[3]   An exception to the exception is bar 19 of Mozart's Symphony no. 36 ("Linz"), movement 1, where only the violins have the thirty-second-note pickup to beat 2. In this case the impulse of the beat gesture coincides with the sounding beat, preceded by the short pickup.

the arm begins the ascent while the hand continues descending, which creates opposition of the two and conflict with the sounds. See video demonstration B.1.

Divisi String Sections

Two-part divisi passages are usually best divided by stand, outside person playing the top line and inside the bottom. Three- or four-part divisis are acoustically strongest if the players of each line are situated as close as possible to each other. Thus for a three-part divisi the top line is played by the first third of the section, the middle line by the middle third, and the bottom line by the back third.

Eyes

It is undeniably easier to hear all the sounds with eyes closed. But there is also a benefit to having eye contact with musicians, as conducting with closed eyes may create an uncomfortable sense of detachment. It is less likely to be off-putting if the conductor is truly connecting with the sounds, but with any whiff of choreography it will not be received well. And even the most genuinely motivated closed-eyes conductor is well advised to keep regular periodic eye contact with the musicians.

Hemiola

In most cases it is advisable not to conform the gesture to the hemiola but to maintain the continuing metric organization. A hemiola is a temporary organization of triple metric values into duple (or less often duple values into triple), which increases energy by creating metric conflict. Conducting the hemiola—in other words, reorganizing the pattern to synch with the temporary reorganization of beats—tends to lessen the conflict and thus reduce the energy surge.[4]

Ictus

Some conducting instruction refers to an "ictus" or a "click," a small atemporal spasm in the wrist designed to demarcate the beginning of a beat

---

[4]   It can be appropriate to conduct the hemiola in passages in which the hemiola is sufficiently strong or extended, for example in the first movement of Tchaikovsky's *Serenade for Strings*, bars 130, 132, and 134–37.

with clarity. Such a motion has limited value at best. As our influence comes from conforming the gesture to the sounds, and as there is no atemporal sound in music, an atemporal spasm disassociates the gesture from the sound and thus limits the conductor's influence. Without an internal structure in the beat gesture, an atemporal "ictus" can at best articulate where the beat began after it has passed.

Intonation

Just as lack of ensemble occurs when musicians do not share the collective sense of pulse, lack of intonation occurs when musicians do not share the collective sense of pitch. Musicians play or sing in tune because they lock into the magical experience of multiple pitches joining into one, and not because they're told "three cents higher," "four cents lower." Musicians generally take responsibility for playing in tune with their colleagues. Especially in fine orchestras, small groups of woodwind and brass players are often found onstage outside of rehearsal time tuning chords or octaves.

A problem of faulty intonation may get solved simply by asking the musicians to listen more carefully for pitch. It is also common to build the chord note by note, either up from the lowest tone or by function: root, then fifth, then third. Although it is easier to hear upper pitches in context of a bass pitch, because we listen up in register for balance it may ultimately be most productive for the musicians to listen up for pitch as well: with the highest tone sustaining, have the remaining musicians produce their pitch when they hear it in their heads. Singing can help a younger instrumental ensemble play in tune: almost always they will be able to sing beautifully in tune, and if so then they are better able to play in tune. If the issue is limited to a small number of experienced musicians, it may well be most effective to ask them to go over the spot themselves outside of rehearsal. Finally, keep in mind that professional musicians take particular responsibility for playing in tune individually and with their colleagues, so address it with sensitivity.

Morale

Musicians' feeling of well-being is vital to an ensemble's effectiveness. The function of rehearsing is to maximize the quality of the experience in the concert, and the quality of performance is an important factor in driving positive morale. Of course for a professional ensemble, pay is also a significant factor, and as in any work or educational environment, respect and a congenial atmosphere are also vital.

Treat the musicians with unflagging respect. Current practice in the United States is to use first names; even as a guest conductor, learn the musicians' first names and use them. It is of course a must for the regular conductor to learn musicians' names.[5] At the same time, be sensitive to the fact that any comment addressed to an individual musician—no matter how constructive—calls that musician out in front of colleagues.[6] It should go without saying not to single out an individual member of the string section or chorus in rehearsal.

Understand too that musicians are artists whose inherent function is to express their individuality to the world, and ensemble playing can be restrictive: musicians are told what to play, how to play it, when to play it, where to play it, how to dress for it, and to do it in lock-step with colleagues. So any opportunity for self-determination is helpful for building and sustaining morale.

Pizzicato

It is perhaps counterintuitive, and counter also to much instruction that calls for sharp beat gestures with pizzicato notes, but passages of extended pizzicato often call for legato gestures. Keep in mind in balancing pizzicato chords that lower pitches are more resonant (and thus louder) than higher pitches; keep in mind in matching articulations with non-string instruments that pizzicato tones may actually last longer than might be expected.

Rehearsal Do's and Don'ts

Do begin the rehearsal by reading through an entire movement or similarly large section, even with limited rehearsal time. This allows you to take stock of the strengths of the ensemble as well as of issues major and minor that need attention. It allows you to "rehearse with your hands," showing phrase shapes, relative dynamics, articulations, balances, intonation corrections, and so on. It allows the musicians to get accustomed to the way your gestures contact the sounds. And not least, it gives the musicians an important sense of how the whole unfolds.

Do vary the rehearsal. Rehearsing requires stopping, but stopping is potentially irritating, and frequent stopping can become tedious. It is

---

[5]   A musician in a major orchestra referring to the music director said to me, "The SOB was here for thirteen years and never called me anything but 'second clarinet.'"

[6]   John de Lancie, the longtime principal oboist of the Philadelphia Orchestra, told me he particularly appreciated that Eugene Ormandy never said a word to him in rehearsal.

advisable to change things up: alternate working out local details with playing longer passages; stop to address a single issue, but also where possible
address two or three.

Don't make a musical request or suggestion without the musicians
experiencing it. If you suggest an improved inflection, balance, or sound
quality, for example, allow the musicians to hear the difference. In most
cases, a verbal comment alone will be meaningless.

Don't ask more than twice. Musicians want to perform their best, but
they do not want to feel inadequate. A good rule of thumb: if you ask for
something in rehearsal and it doesn't happen, ask again, once. If it doesn't
happen a second time move on, as it isn't going to happen and to pursue it
only makes the musician feel bad.

Working with professional string players, do consult with the concertmaster and principals on issues of bowing and sound quality. Even for a
conductor who is a skilled string player with an instinctive understanding
of sound production, it is generally best to avoid offering specific technical
advice to professional musicians. Instead, describe the desired result to the
concertmaster or section leader and leave it to them to make specific technical suggestions to the section. It is their job, they probably know it better
than you, and it helps foster an environment of mutual respect. On the
other hand, however, conductors of amateur choruses and less advanced
instrumental ensembles have a responsibility to address technical issues.

Rudeness from Musicians

It is the rare and fortunate conductor who never encounters a rude remark
or other bad behavior in rehearsal. Human instinct is to feel attacked by
the entire ensemble, but it is likely that the other musicians find the behavior equally inappropriate. If ignoring it is not possible, a self-deprecating
humorous comment is the best response.

String Chords of Three or Four Parts

In music of the seventeenth and eighteenth centuries, string chords of
three or four tones were intended to be rolled from the bottom up.[7] With
a modern preference for strict simultaneities, string players commonly
divide such chords, outside players on the upper two tones and inside players on the lower two. As a result, only half the section plays the uppermost

---

[7]   It is a popular misconception that the instruments had flatter bridges, which allowed the simultaneous sounding of three or even four tones.

tone, which usually has melodic priority. If the chords are not rolled, keeping the entire section on the upper two tones is almost always the better solution, as the lower tones are usually covered or acoustically implied by other instruments.

Speaking from the Stage

With audiences increasingly unfamiliar with classical music, the conductor may well take a role in maximizing the experience by speaking from the stage. However, what to say and when to say it is important. A stage talk might include descriptions of the works, interesting facts about the composer, or an explanation of the construction of the program; in other words, information that opens a listener's ear to the experience. And humor is generally welcome. It is best though to avoid specific things to listen for, as the listener focused on that event loses the possibility of the experience available from absorbing all the sounds.

The conscious experience of speaking from the stage is very different from that of conducting a profound work of art; similarly, the experience of listening to a talk about music is profoundly different from experiencing the music. If the music begins directly after a talk, it is harder for both the conductor and the listeners to switch gears and be fully open to the experience. For this reason, a contextual break between the two is recommended: exit the stage while the ensemble tunes or performs some otherwise mechanical operation or lighting change. This buffer allows time for the material of the talk to recede and for the ears of the audience and the performers to turn fully to the sounds.

An exception, however, is with a new work in a challenging musical language. Playing excerpts from the work with introductory remarks directly prior to the performance may well enhance the experience.

Triple Legato Uneven Beat

An uneven beat is useful for passages too slow to conduct in large note values and not slow enough to conduct in smaller ones. Typically this occurs in music in a triple legato character, often in the course of slowing down.

For example, consider a passage in triple legato character, notated in dotted half notes. If it is too slow to give a single beat for the dotted half note yet not slow enough to give continuing quarter-note beats, it is possible to give an uneven beat: a quarter-note beat followed by a half-note beat. Quarter-note one gets a small duple legato beat with a small eighth-note ascent and a similarly small descent to quarter-note two; quarter-notes two and three join to form a single duple legato half-note beat, in which the ascent and descent each take the space of a single quarter note. Both segments of the dotted half-note gesture begin at the same point.

Different Genres

Accompanying

Know the Score

Conducting an accompaniment is similar to conducting an ensemble work: the conductor is the conduit between the musicians onstage, including the soloist. While a solo work may seem like an opportunity for less intensive preparation, in fact it involves an extra layer of preparation. The deeper the conductor's understanding of both solo and accompaniment parts, the easier it becomes to assist their connection.

Make It Work for the Soloist

A solo work is about featuring the soloist, and in all likelihood that person has invested more time and energy and experience with it than the conductor. Ideally you will be in synch with your soloists and will take inspiration from them. If you find yourself at odds, your responsibility is to make the soloist's vision work to the extent possible.

Don't Follow the Soloist

Don't follow the soloist; rather, conform your gestures to the sounds, guiding the person to respond to the sounds as you would a musician in the ensemble. It may help to think of leading your soloists in what they want to do.

Don't Stop

In the case of a soloist's memory slip in concert, if at all possible do not stop. Accompanying musicians may well recognize added or skipped bars, and with luck order will be restored.

Smile

Soloists are under considerable pressure. Respond to them warmly, make them feel comfortable, and don't be afraid to smile.

Mark the Rests

Counting rests accurately can be challenging for the musicians, especially if the soloist's rhythm is flexible. It is often best to stop conducting completely during extended passages for soloist alone. But when in doubt mark the rests, traveling through the pattern with the wrist and clearly indicating the downbeats.

Baroque Music

Baroque music presents challenges foreign to later orchestral works, including whether to use harpsichord, ornamentation, and final ritardandos. Much Baroque music does not require a conductor; such works may be better left unconducted. Playing without a conductor offers musicians responsibility, an increased commitment to ensemble playing by hearing, and a heightened sense of pride.

Harpsichord

In Baroque times heat was expensive, rooms were small, rehearsal was minimal, and string instruments—with gut strings and convex bows—were soft. A harpsichord served perfectly to keep the group together and to fill in inner voices. In current concert conditions, the downside of including a harpsichord may well outweigh the upside.

The biggest challenge presented by the harpsichord is balance. A single-manual harpsichord has a minimal range of volume, effected solely by adding or subtracting the number of notes played; modern string sections and wind instruments have a much larger range of volume. If audible in soft tutti passages, the harpsichord is likely inaudible in loud passages, resulting in a fundamental and musically unwarranted change in texture.

A second problem is the divergent sound quality between the harpsichord and the other string and wind instruments. The dry plucked string sound of a harpsichord is quite different from the sustained sound of strings and winds. Modern harpsichords have been constructed to maximize volume, as have modern string instruments: the louder the instruments, the greater the divergence in sound quality.

Double-manual harpsichords can overcome some of the challenges by virtue of greater range, resonance, and sound color; however, single-manual instruments are more common. Given modern standards of rehearsal and performance, a harpsichord is no longer necessary to maintain ensemble; you may prefer to use one only if it is needed to fill in harmonies (rare) or has dedicated solos, such as in the final movement of Haydn's Symphony no. 98.

Ornamentation

Library shelves are filled with volumes about performing ornaments in Baroque and Classical Era music. While it is undoubtedly helpful to be aware of and fluent in the possibilities, ultimately the decision of how to ornament a single tone should come down to this simple consideration: how it sounds best.

For practical purposes, large ensembles are generally limited to relatively simple ornaments of single tones. Extended solos, however, call for more intricate ornamentation. The practice of ornamenting extended solos originates from a need to sustain tones. Harpsichords and Baroque bows were incapable of sustaining to the degree that pianos and modern concave bows are; ornaments are additional notes that sustain the line without changing the harmony. Instrumentalists may well provide their own ornamentation, but the conductor may be called on. Example B.1 presents movement 2 of Handel's "Water Music," *Suite in F Major* (HWV 348), with both Handel's original oboe line and an ornamented version of my own creation.[8]

Example B.1. Handel, "Water Music," *Suite in F Major*, mvt. 2.

(continued)

---

[8]   Use of this ornamented version in performance is freely granted.

Example B.1.—*(concluded)*

Critical to a successful ornamentation is that the varied rhythms and pitches reinforce the structure of energy of the original. In Handel's original the energy grows from the tonicized D minor (bar 3) through the tonicizations of F major (bar 6) and G major (bar 8) to the climactic diminished 7th downbeat of bar 9. Energy is released from bar 9 to the A major downbeat of bar 10. The ornamentation reinforces the structure of energy with an increase in rhythmic density to bar 9 followed by a subtle decrease of rhythmic density to the middle of bar 10.

From bar 10 energy grows through tonicizations of C major (bar 13) and D minor (bar 15) to the climax of the movement at the downbeat of bar 16, and then is released to bar 18. Ornamentation reinforces this structure of energy with increasing rhythmic density and the appoggiatura at bar 16.

A third, less pronounced growth of energy occurs from bar 18 to the downbeat of bar 23; it is released over the ensuing six bars, with secondary injections of impulse in bars 28 and 30 before the final cadence. The ornamented version reinforces the secondary impulses in bars 28 and 30, and highlights the surprise forte VI 6 (bar 31) with an octave ascent mimicking the octave ascent of bar 14, before returning to the lower octave of the final dominant harmony.

Final Ritardandos

Due to the constancy of tempo and material in Baroque movements, many performers approach the final few bars with a pronounced ritardando. This is a legitimate response to the requirement of releasing energy by slowing the tempo, but an overly broad ritardando separates those final tones metrically from the body of the movement. Performers would do well to hear the release of energy in the final extended passage in the home key and to allow the tempo to settle accordingly, obviating any need for a pronounced pullback at the very end.

Opera Conducting

Opera provides an aesthetic experience fundamentally different from that of pure music, thus opera conducting has a different set of responsibilities and challenges. Opera is first and foremost an experience of theater, heightened by music and offering a vehicle for voices to shine. Singers have a wide array of responsibilities: singing and acting and moving around the stage. Thus the conductor's responsibilities above and beyond maximizing the musical possibilities include setting tempos that incorporate the singers' breath control, ensuring that the orchestra doesn't overbalance the voices (particularly challenging, as musicians in the pit and singers onstage are limited in what they can hear of each other), and above all ensuring that the singers make their entrances, which means maintaining eye contact and forming beat gestures high enough for them to see.

Opera conducting also requires a different, more extensive preparation process. It includes learning the text thoroughly (likely requiring a degree of fluency in a foreign language) and reaching an understanding of the dramatic unfolding, scene by scene, aria by aria.

It also requires security with the accompanied recitatives. These can be particularly challenging physical exercises, as absent a continuum of the pulse in a musical context it is easy to get behind or otherwise to lose the singer. As a practical matter, if the vocal rhythm is particularly elastic, it may be appropriate to mark the pattern quickly through an extended rest and wait for the soloist to catch up before preparing the next orchestral entrance. Secco recitatives (accompanied by continuo only) are best left unconducted if possible.

Accompanying opera singers and other vocal soloists can be subtly different than accompanying instrumentalists. While instrumental soloists will likely come to the process with a firm vision of tempo, articulations, character, and so on, singers tend to expect and want more active direction from the podium. As with instrumentalists, do not follow the singers but conform your gestures to their sounds, guiding them to what they want to do.

As a reminder, the descent is critical in helping an ensemble coalesce at the beginning of a beat. Singers routinely stretch impressive notes to project the beauty and grandeur of their voices. As the singer stretches, stretch the ascent; in other words, keep going up. The singer will invariably give some indication of when the next beat will begin; form the descent in accordance with the tempo and character of the ensuing beat.

BIBLIOGRAPHY

Alcantara, Pedro de. *Indirect Procedures: A Musician's Guide to the Alexander Technique*. 2nd ed. New York: Oxford University Press, 2013.

Alcantara, Pedro de. *Integrated Practice: Coordination, Rhythm and Sound*. New York: Oxford University Press, 2011.

Berry, Wallace. *Musical Structure and Performance*. New Haven, CT: Yale University Press, 1989.

Carney, Dana R., Amy J. C. Cuddy, and Andy J. Yap. "Power Posing: Brief Nonverbal Displays Affect Neuroendocrine Levels and Risk Tolerance." *Psychological Science* 21, no. 10 (October 2010): 1363–68.

Cone, Edward T. *Musical Form and Musical Performance*. New York: Norton, 1968.

Cuddy, Amy J. C., Peter Glick, and Anna Beninger. "The Dynamics of Warmth and Competence Judgments, and Their Outcomes in Organizations." *Research in Organizational Behavior* 31 (2011): 73–98.

Dunsby, Jonathan. "Guest Editorial: Performance and Analysis of Music." *Music Analysis* 8 (March–July 1989): 5–20.

Ferrer, Emilio, and Jonathan L. Helm. "Dynamical Systems Modeling of Physiological Coregulation in Dyadic Interactions." *International Journal of Psychophysiology* 88 (2013): 296–308.

Helm, Jonathan L., David Sbarra, and Emilio Ferrer. "Assessing Cross-Partner Associations in Physiological Responses via Coupled Oscillator Models." *Emotion* 12 (2009): 748–62.

Meyer, Leonard B. *Explaining Music: Essays and Explorations*. Berkeley: University of California Press, 1973.

Miyake, Yoshihiro. "Co-creation Systems: Ma and Communication." In *Culture and Neural Frames of Cognition and Communication*, edited by Shihui Han and Ernst Pöppel, 139–52. Heidelberg: Springer, 2011.

Muscle Premium [computer program]. *Visible Body*. Newton, MA: Argosy Publishing, 2007–15. www.visiblebody.com.

Rink, John. "Analysis and (or?) Performance." In *Musical Performance: A Guide to Understanding*, edited by John Rink, 35–58. Cambridge: Cambridge University Press, 2002.

Schachter, Carl. "20th-Century Analysis and Mozart Performance." *Early Music* 19, no. 4, *Performing Mozart's Music I* (November 1991): 620–26.

Stein, Erwin. *Form and Performance*. New York: Knopf, 1962.

Thakar, Markand. *Counterpoint: Fundamentals of Music Making*. New Haven, CT: Yale University Press, 1990.

———. *Looking for the "Harp" Quartet: An Investigation into Musical Beauty.* Rochester, NY: University of Rochester Press, 2011.

Vineyard, Missy. *How You Stand, How You Move, How You Live: Learning the Alexander Technique to Explore Your Mind-Body Connection and Achieve Self-Mastery*. New York: Marlowe, 2007.

INDEX

"What distinguishes Markand Thakar as a conductor and a teacher is the unique balance that he achieves between the technical and the emotional contents of music, and his ability to communicate that balance to both audiences and students. It is this quality that runs throughout Thakar's book, and it is this quality that makes the book both different from others and extraordinarily valuable."

—Henry Fogel, dean, Chicago College of Performing Arts, Roosevelt University

"With insight into how mind and body contribute effectively to the conductor's presentation, *On the Principles and Practice of Conducting* offers a fresh and highly detailed approach to successful music making from the podium. As an added plus, the online video demonstrations clearly solve a multitude of technical issues confronting conductors. A must read for all students of conducting!"

—David Effron, professor of orchestral conducting, Jacobs School of Music, Indiana University

Printed in the United States
by Baker & Taylor Publisher Services